COCKADOODLEDOOO!        WASSAT?

# SUPER SUMMER FUN

**Created by OWL Magazine**
Edited by Laima Dingwall and Annabel Slaight

 **An OWL Magazine/Golden Press® Book**

Canadian ISBN 0-919872-87-5
U.S. ISBN 0-307-13728-7    A B C D E F G H I J

Published in Canada by Greey de Pencier Books, Toronto
Originally published as THE OWL FUN BOOK, 1982

Canadian Cataloguing in Publication Data
Main entry under title:
**SUPER SUMMER FUN**
Previous ed. had title the OWL Fun Book.
ISBN 0-919872-87-5

1. Amusements — Juvenile literature. I. Slaight, Annabel, 1940-    II. Dingwall, Laima, 1953-
III. OWL (Toronto, Ont.). IV. Title: The OWL fun book.
GV1203.094 1984   j790.1-922   C83-098583-2

# CONTENTS

LOOK AT ALL THAT STUFF TO DO!

I THINK I'LL MAKE A BOAT.

I CAN NEVER MAKE MY MIND UP.

This is the second big fun-filled book that we at OWL, the Discovery Magazine for Children, have created just for you. We've been hard at work thinking of ideas to help you make the most of summer ever since we finished writing *OWL'S Winter Fun* book that so many of you said made your winter sparkle.

If you haven't seen *OWL'S Winter Fun* book, look for it in a store or library. James Houston's award-winning adventure about two Inuit (Eskimo) children and their narrow escape from ''Long Claws'' should leave you breathless. And we're sure that you'll also enjoy all the great puzzles, activities, colorful animal pictures and some wonderful paintings showing winter on Mars.

But now you're ready to begin *OWL'S Summer Fun* book. We hope it will keep you entertained from the first day you leave your gloves inside to the last day the leaves fly. If you do all the puzzles, finish all the things to make, look at all the beautiful pictures, chuckle at all the jokes and read the two wonderful stories (including some spooky science fiction by Monica Hughes), you should be busy for weeks.

There are pages filled with rainy day activities, lots of weird things to do when you're so bored you don't know what to do, and there's a word search that takes hours to complete. Want to know what different clouds mean or how to make some clouds of your own? Or would you like some simple instructions for building a real telegraph set? Or perhaps you'd like to discover how to build the world's best paper airplane or how to grow a yummy garden. We've even given you our best ideas for keeping cool. Turn the page to let the fun begin...

THIS BOOK GIVES YOU METRIC AND IMPERIAL MEASUREMENTS. GREAT, EH?

YESSIR.

YESSIR.

# Be a "Signs of Summer" Detective

The scene on this page was drawn one month earlier than the scene on the opposite page. How many things are different? We found 14, but maybe you can find more. Most of the changes are signs that spring has turned to summer. For example, the early flowers have disappeared and the tulips are in full bloom. How good a detective are you?

*Answers on page 128*

9

# A Closer Look at Clouds

Above the clouds the sun is always shining and the sky is always blue. When you're in a plane, the clouds look like something you could touch. Of course, you can't.

To see how a cloud is made, hold your mouth close to a mirror and blow softly. When your warm moist breath hits the cold glass, it condenses into tiny water droplets. This rapid cooling of water vapor is what creates clouds in the sky.

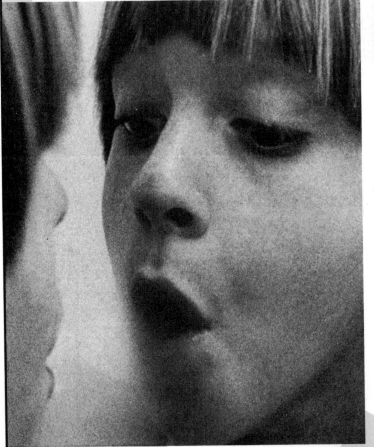

To discover which way the wind is blowing the clouds, you can build a nephoscope like the one here. It is simply a small mirror mounted on a piece of cardboard marked with the compass directions. Use a compass to help you match N on your nephoscope with north. Then watch the reflection of the clouds on the mirror.

Clouds are made of billions of tiny water droplets (or ice crystals when it's cold) floating in the air. There are over 6 trillion of them in the average-sized thundercloud.

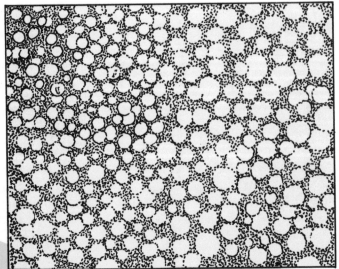

Here's another way to make a cloud of your own. By blowing through a straw into the cup of piping hot water you can create an updraft of warm, moist air. When it meets the cool pie plate — presto! a cloud is formed.

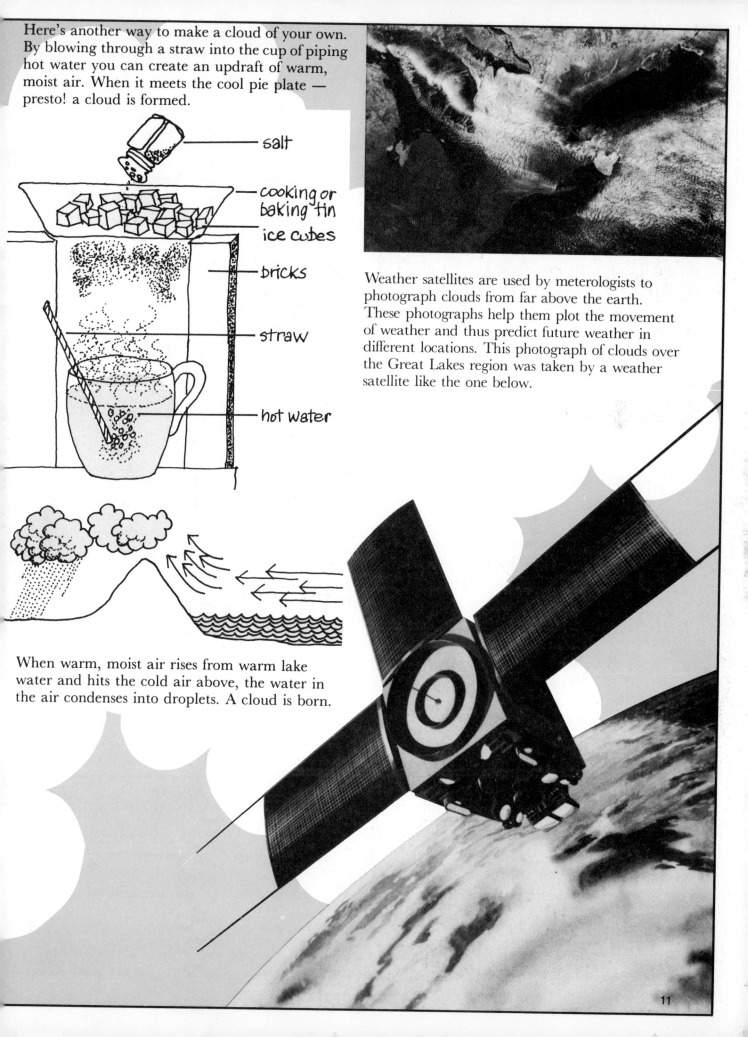

salt

cooking or baking tin

ice cubes

bricks

straw

hot water

When warm, moist air rises from warm lake water and hits the cold air above, the water in the air condenses into droplets. A cloud is born.

Weather satellites are used by meterologists to photograph clouds from far above the earth. These photographs help them plot the movement of weather and thus predict future weather in different locations. This photograph of clouds over the Great Lakes region was taken by a weather satellite like the one below.

# Ho! Ho! Ho!

Q. What is black and white and has 16 wheels?
A. A zebra on roller skates.

Q. What did the ground say to the rain?
A. "If you keep that up, my name will be mud."

Q. Why can't a bicycle stand by itself?
A. Because it's two tired.

Q. What is black and white and red all over?
A. A penguin with a sunburn.

Q. What kind of beans will never grow in a garden?
A. Jellybeans.

Q. What bird is present at every meal?
A. A swallow.

Q. Why is the letter A like honeysuckle?
A. Because a B always follows it.

Q. How do you keep milk from turning sour?
A. Leave it in the cow.

Q. What insect would make the best outfielder?
A. A spider — it's great at catching flies.

Q. What are the largest ants in the world?
A. Elephants.

Q. Why are days long in summer and short in winter?
A. Heat expands things and cold contracts them.

Q. What spends the summer in a fur coat?
A. A moth.

Q. What did the mayonnaise say to the refrigerator?
A. "Please close the door — I'm dressing."

Q. How do you know the ocean is friendly?
A. Because it waves.

Q. What is kept in an air-conditioned vault?
A. Cold cash.

Q. What is it that's got a heart in its head?
A. Lettuce.

Q. What bird is a thief?
A. A robin.

Q. What do you call a frightened skin diver?
A. Chicken of the sea.

Q. Why did the busy bee call the flowers lazy?
A. Because they were always in bed.

Q. Why did the greenhouse call the doctor?
A. It had window panes.

Q. What has 18 legs, red spots and catches flies?
A. A baseball team with measles.

Q. What is the first thing you put in a garden?
A. Your foot.

Q. Why is a cat like the sun?
A. They both go out at night.

Q. What do you call a sunburn on your stomach?
A. A pot roast.

I DON'T GET IT!

?

Q. Why did the dog lie out in the sun?
A. He wanted to become a hot dog.

Q. What does every cat get when it takes to the water?
A. Wet.

Q. What did the salad say to the spoon and fork?
A. "You get me all mixed up."

Q. What kind of fish do you find in a bird cage?
A. Perch.

Q. Why do fish hate tennis?
A. They don't want to get too close to the net.

Q. What happens when you give a cat lemonade?
A. You get a sour puss.

# Be a Cloud Detective

Rate yourself as a cloud detective. See how many of the different clouds shown here you can match up with the clues below. Write the numbers opposite the clues.

### Cirrus
Very high, thin, wispy clouds usually formed by ice crystals. When they begin to cover the whole sky there is an 80 per cent chance of rain in the next 24 hours.

### Cirrocumulus
High, thin layers of bright white clouds that look like ripples on the beach. They indicate continued fair weather.

### Altocumulus
A high layer of many tightly packed cloudlets. Usually means rain is to follow in eight to ten hours.

### Cumulonimbus
A towering, high, thick cloud that's dark grey in the center. This is a developing storm cloud and may be accompanied by large raindrops or even hail.

### Thunderhead
A mushroom-shaped cloud with a flat top. Usually marks the site of an intense thunderstorm.

### Fair weather cumulus
Fluffy white clouds with rounded tops. If they are small and float lazily along, they mean continued good weather.

**Mammotocumulus**
Tiny, rounded clouds on the undersurface of a thick layer of clouds. Indicate stormy weather with wind and rain very soon.

Using some of the information on these pages you can predict the weather. Just like a weatherman, you will not always be right, but if you keep a record of what kinds of clouds you see and what kind of weather comes in the next 24 hours, your accuracy will improve.

How do you rate as a cloud detective?
Perfect score - super
4 to 6 clouds identified - good
Under 4 clouds identified - better luck next time.

*Answers on page 128*

# Holiday Crossword

**Clues**

*Across:*

1. Outdoor meals on sunny days
5. Where the sea meets the land
7. A dandy flower
10. If you _ _ _ in the sun too long, you'll get burnt.
12. Do this in water with a mask and breathing tube.
13. A small freshwater fish often used as bait
16. Ice cream is fun to _ _ _ .
19. You could use *13 across* when you go _ _ _ _ _ _ _ .
21. Look for one of these on a beach.
23. A honey-maker
24. Water will _ _ _ _ _ _ _ _ _ in a dish in the sun.
25. Always dive into _ _ _ _ water.

*Down:*

1. You _ _ _ _ _ _ a canoe.
2. You'll need *1 down* if you have one of these.
3. Add this to drinks on a hot day.
4. A very wet activity
5. It's hot, bright and far away.
6. It's got two wheels and pedals.
8. Fill it up with sand on the beach.
9. Taking _ _ _ _ _ _ _ instead of baths saves water.
11. Another name for *8 down*
12. What goes up and down, backwards and forwards?
14. A soap _ _ _ _ _ _ pops easily.
15. In a boat always wear a _ _ _ _ jacket.
17. A life guard usually sits on a high _ _ _ _ _ _ .
18. A slippery thing found in a playground.
20. This contains eggs in spring, babies in summer.
22. The top of it is usually covered with hair.

*Answers on page 128*

# Super Summer Activities

It's super when you can swing in a hammock

...and spend day after day doing mostly anything you like.

LES ETOILES DE St HUBERT

What would you like to do most?

# DR. ZED'S FANTASTIC FLASHLIGHT!

To make your flashlight you will need:
two 1.5 volt batteries
masking tape
a sharp knife, and an adult to help you
a single strand of thin, plastic-covered bell wire,
   12 cm/5 in. long
a 3 volt bulb and bulb holder

1. Tape the batteries together, positive to negative.

2. Connect the batteries, bell wire and bulb as in the illustration.

3. Press the bulb holder down on the positive end of the battery to turn your flashlight on.

# DR.ZED'S HUM-DINGER-DOOR-BUZZER

To make your buzzer you'll need:
two 1.5 volt batteries
masking tape
a rubber band
three single strands of thin, plastic-covered bell wire, 2m/6 ft. long

a sharp knife, and an adult to help you
a 3 volt buzzer (you can buy one at a hardware store)
a push button (you can buy one at a hardware store)

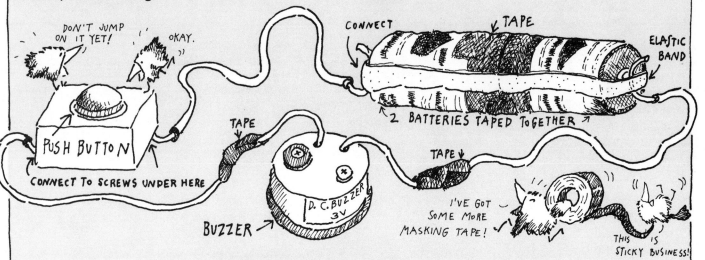

1. Tape the batteries together, positive to negative. Keep them pressed together with an elastic band.

2. Using a sharp knife, peel 1.5 cm/½ in. of plastic off both ends of each piece of bell wire.

3. Connect the batteries, push button and buzzer together as in the illustration.

4. Tape the push button on the frame outside your door, and the buzzer and batteries inside. Make sure to tape the bell wire flat so that it doesn't get in the way when you open the door.

# DR. ZED'S TERRIFIC TAP-TAP-TAP TELEGRAPH SET

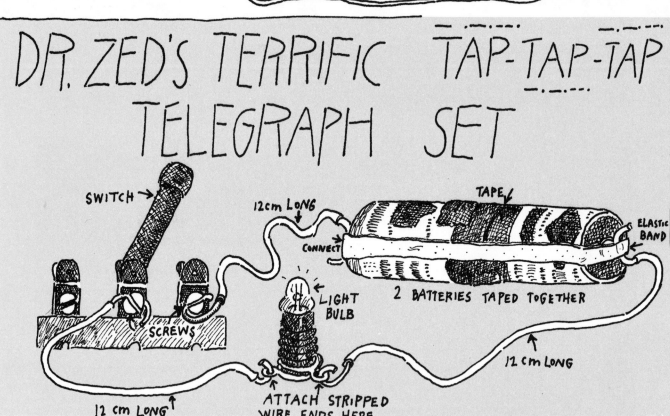

SWITCH →

12cm LONG ↓

TAPE ↓

CONNECT

ELASTIC BAND ←

LIGHT BULB ←

2 BATTERIES TAPED TOGETHER

SCREWS

12 cm LONG ↑

12 cm LONG ↑

ATTACH STRIPPED WIRE ENDS HERE

To make your telegraph set you will need:
two 1.5 volt batteries
masking tape
a rubber band
a sharp knife, and an adult to help you
three single strands of thin, plastic-covered bell
    wire, 12 cm/5 in. long
a 3 volt bulb and bulb holder
a switch (you can buy one at a hardware store)

1. Tape the batteries together, positive to negative. Keep them pressed together with a rubber band.

2. Using a sharp knife, peel 1/5 cm/½ in. of plastic off both ends of each piece of bell wire.

3. Connect the batteries, push button and buzzer together as in the illustration.

4. To operate your telegraph, simply move the switch up and down to turn the light on and off.

# MORSE CODE

a ·—
b —···
c —·—·
d —··
e ·
f ··—·
g ——·
h ····
i ··
j ·———
k —·—
l ·—··
m ——
n —·
o ———
p ·——·
q ——·—
r ·—·

s ···
t —
u ··—
v ···—
w ·——
x —··—
y —·——
z ——··

1 ·————
2 ··———
3 ···——
4 ····—
5 ·····
6 —····
7 ——···
8 ———··
9 ————·
0 —————

BEGINNING OF TRANSMISSION— — · — · —
END OF TRANSMISSION— · — · — ·
ERROR— · · · · · · · ·

THE CIRCLES IN THE CODE ARE CALLED DOTS AND THE LINES ARE CALLED DASHES!

FLIP SWITCH QUICKLY FOR DOTS AND HOLD DOWN LONGER FOR DASHES!

HOW CLEVER!

WE CAN SUBSTITUTE A BUZZER FOR THE LIGHT AND MAKE A WONDERFULLY NOISY TELEGRAPH SET!

GREAT!

OH YEAH!

I BET IF WE HAD 2 SETS AND LONGER WIRES, WE COULD SEND MESSAGES TO AND FROM DIFFERENT ROOMS!!

# DR. ZED'S ELECTRIFYING QUIZ GAME

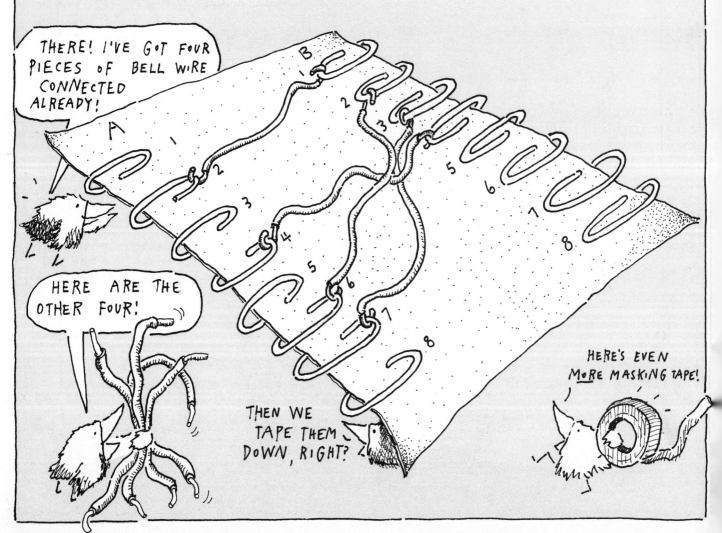

To make your quiz game you will need:
16 paper clips
a 21 cm by 26 cm/8 in. by 10 in. piece of
   cardboard
a single strand of thin, plastic-covered bell wire,
   4 m/13 ft. long
scissors
a sharp knife, and an adult to help you

masking tape
a piece of paper
a pencil
two 1.5 volt batteries
an elastic band
a 3 volt bulb and bulb holder

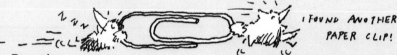

I FOUND ANOTHER PAPER CLIP!

*Making the Game Board*
1. Attach 8 paper clips to each side of the cardboard as in the illustration. Put an A above the clips on the left side, a B on the right. Number the clips from 1 to 8 on both sides of the cardboard.
2. Cut eight 30 cm/12 in.-long pieces of bell wire. With a sharp knife, peel 1.5 cm/½ in. of plastic off the ends of each piece of bell wire.
3. With the bell wire, make the following connections between the clips on side A and B of the cardboard:

| Side A | Side B |
|--------|--------|
| 1 | 6 |
| 2 | 1 |
| 3 | 7 |
| 4 | 4 |
| 5 | 8 |
| 6 | 2 |
| 7 | 3 |
| 8 | 5 |

4. Turn the cardboard over so the wires are on the bottom.

5. Trace the pictures of animals on the next page or draw your own and clip them onto the left side of the cardboard. Trace the pictures of their feet and clip them to the other side. Make sure the circuits match, for instance — if the rabbit is on clip 1, its feet should be on clip 6 (see instruction 3).

*Making the Flasher*
1. Tape the batteries together, positive to negative. Keep them pressed together with an elastic band.
2. Cut three 10 cm/4 in.-long pieces of bell wire. Peel 1.5 cm/½ in. of plastic off each end.
3. Connect the batteries, bell wire and bulb holder together as in the illustration.

*Turn the Animals Face Up and Play*
Touch one of the free ends of the bell wire to an animal. Touch the other bell wire to the foot you think it matches. If you're correct the light should flash on.

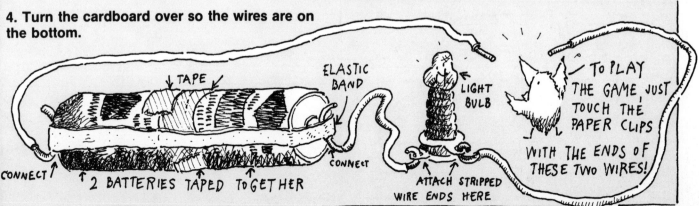

CONNECT   TAPE   ELASTIC BAND   LIGHT BULB   TO PLAY THE GAME, JUST TOUCH THE PAPER CLIPS WITH THE ENDS OF THESE TWO WIRES!

2 BATTERIES TAPED TOGETHER   CONNECT   ATTACH STRIPPED WIRE ENDS HERE

# Holiday Word Search

All the words in this puzzle are things you can do or see this summer, as well as things you can read about in this book. We've started it for you by drawing a line around "waves" and striking it off the list. Do the same with the other words, but be careful because they can run in any direction and can also cross and overlap. When you've circled all the words in the puzzle, the letters that remain will spell out some amazing facts about raindrops.

```
C I S R E P P I L F S E O T I U Q S O M T
L T I S S T N O O T T B A S E B A L L S
O R U E E R T H O A E F T F A L L I A N E
U G R K C A P K C A B I C Y C L E S A I L
D N D O Y D R O C P S N D N I W R N H A B
S R E J R R S H H S A S P E A E G O S E B
D S L I A E K E R U T N E V D A N R I D E
C I N C I P E T E M A R E E S S I K F I P
M A L A D U L R H M A S E N I N G E R L D
R N O P C S S A O E R F U D G E G L A S E
R R E O U K E N T R D S F U N D O I T R S
D E W D H I S T A R S L E L I E J N S E T
A T R G R U N E I D O W N E R T S G A T N
S A R E S A H B R M A P I E E E D L I A E
T W A S P S G I D K Y E H M E C A M C W M
C R B U R N B G D N E T R B T T U T N S I
E E T H I E Y A E R A E H F N I I L A T R
S D O M N P U Z Z L E S T G E V H N E B E
N N M O T R T O R M A N D R I E O E U N P
I U D E D O O N D T H E T T R M A S K O X
H I K I N G P L A Y F L Y T O M A T O P E
```

| | | | | | | |
|---|---|---|---|---|---|---|
| ACTIVITY | CLOUDS | FINS | HOT | NEST | SALT | SUPERDART |
| ADVENTURE | COOL | FLIPPERS | HUMMINGBIRD | ORIENTEERING | SAND | SWIM |
| AIR | DETECTIVE | FLY | INSECTS | PEBBLES | SNACKS | TOMATO |
| BACKPACK | DIARY | FUDGE | JOGGING | PICNIC | SNORKELING | UNDERWATER |
| BASEBALL | DIG | FUN | JOKES | PLAY | STARFISH | WASPS |
| BEACH | DR. ZED | GARDEN | MASK | PUZZLES | STARS | WATER SLIDE |
| BICYCLES | EXPERIMENTS | GORP | MIGHTY MITES | RIDE | SUMMER | WAVES |
| BIRDS | FEEDER | HIKING | MOSQUITOES | RUN | SUN | WIND |

**A Helpful Hint: starting at the top left hand corner of the puzzle and moving from left to right, jot down the leftover letters in the order they appear.**

The hidden amazing facts are:

\_ \_ \_ \_ \_ \_ \_ \_ \_ \_ \_ \_ \_ \_ \_ \_ \_ \_     \_ \_ \_ \_ \_ \_ \_ \_ \_ \_ \_ \_ \_ \_ \_ \_ \_ \_ \_

\_ \_ \_ \_ \_ \_ \_ \_ \_ \_ \_ \_ \_ \_ \_ \_ \_ \_ \_     \_ \_ \_ \_ \_ \_ \_ \_ \_ \_ \_ \_ \_ \_ \_ \_ \_ \_

\_ \_ \_ \_ \_ \_ \_ \_ \_ \_ \_ \_ \_ \_ \_ \_ \_     \_ \_ \_ \_ \_ \_ \_ \_ \_ \_ \_ \_ \_ \_ \_ \_ \_

# Summer Around the World

If you are celebrating summer right now, you can bet that someone on the other side of the world is probably shivering kneedeep in snow. It's true! But no matter what time of year different seasons come, kids around the world do amazingly similar things. For instance, you can see for yourself what summer is like around the world with this quick tour from Mexico to Thailand and back again.

We go swimming and travel along mountains and highlands.

*Kazuko, , Yoshiko, and Katsumi, Iakeda, 14, 12 and 10, Urawa, Japan*

I ride my bike, play catch and go swimming — in a swimming pool.

*Andre Valee, 11, Leduc, Alberta, Canada*

In Hawaii we do summer things all year round.

*Beth Gartrell, 9, Honolulu, Hawaii*

I love scouting, going on hikes and backpacking. I also enjoy baseball.

*Erik Johnson, 12, Honeyville, Utah, U.S.A.*

We go for day trips on junks in the waters of Hong Kong. Sometimes we take a ferry to an island and walk on beaches.

*Heather A. Woolner, 11, Hong Kong*

I go to the coast and fish for tuna. I collect coral and look at the fish.

*Edward Worsfold, 10, Guadlalajara, Mexico*

Summer here is extremely hot. Near our house are rats, lizards and sometimes snakes. We have a banana tree and coconut tree in our garden. *Sophi Laplane, 12, Bangkok, Thailand*

We swim, play tennis, go to the beach and help with haymaking. We go barefoot a lot.

*Kim and Martyne Steffer, 13 and 11; Philippa and Jane Priest, 12 and 10, Auckland, New Zealand*

I like playing, swimming horseback riding, clambering, climbing and "mucking around" in a sandy-bottomed creek near the beach.

*Deanne Adcock, 10, Gympie, Australia*

I enjoy going to my grandfather's house and out to the field to help stack the bales of hay.

*Ian Crawford, 9, Cloncloghy, Ireland*

We go to the local beach and play games in the sand and climb on the rocks.

*Mark and Sharon Davey, 10 and 8½, Cornwall, England*

The sun shines brightly from 3 a.m. to 11 p.m. every day in the summer. We call the time between sunset and sunrise the summer dim.

*John Robert Irvine, 11, Shetland Island, Scotland*

Summer is the only season of the year when we can have our meals outside in the garden. *Cael Genevieve, 14, La Queue-lez-Yvelines, France*

I go snorkeling with my father out to the coral reef and back in the Gulf of Sirte. *David West, 9½, Tripoli, Libya*

One summer I went to the Red Sea, and we went snorkeling and saw all sorts of fish and coral reefs.

*Naomi Baker, 11, Jerusalem, Israel*

I swim in the Aialian Gulf — the warmest body of water in the world. It's just like bath water.

*Colin Bankam, 9½, Ras Tanura, Saudi Arabia*

I'm a sea scout and enjoy camping trips.

*Allan M. Anderson, 11, Rio de Janeiro, Brazil*

## The Seasons Around The World

|  | North of the Equator | South of the Equator |
|---|---|---|
| Start of Summer | June 21 | December 21 |
| Start of Fall | September 21 | March 21 |
| Start of Winter | December 21 | June 21 |
| Start of Spring | March 21 | September 21 |

31

# Amazing But True

On hot summer days polar bears keep cool by digging down to the permafrost (a layer of earth that is always frozen), then crawling into this refreshing "ice box."

Wallabies use their saliva to keep cool. First a wallaby licks its paws and rubs them over its face. And if this doesn't cool it down, the wallaby sits very still and dribbles all over itself. Dribble, dribble, drip!

Don't feel sorry for a woolly sheep on hot days. If you were to stick your hands inside a sheep's thick fleece you'd find that the wool close to the animal's skin would be cooler than its outermost wool. That's because the sheep's fleece is one of nature's best insulators.

You might not want to rush out of your cozy home once it's started to rain, but a worm certainly would. That's because worms breathe through their skins and if they stay in soggy soil they drown. But when the sun comes out, worms must hurry into the earth again — too much heat can also kill them. What an up and down life!

The California spiny lizard would scorch in the desert if it didn't occasionally crawl under a rock. It has a very unusual way of discovering when it's time to get out of the sun: a hidden third eye in the middle of its forehead tells it when it's time to cool off.

The desert rat has a clever way of staying cool. It avoids the scorching sun by spending the hottest part of the day deep in its underground tunnels. These tunnels have sharp hairpin turns to help keep out the heat.

If all the Earth's oceans evaporated, there'd be enough salt to pile as high as a 50-story building.

There are between two or three million worms under-ground in an area the size of a football field.

Would you like to go swim-ming in a suit of armor? Of course not, and neither does the nine-banded arm-adillo of South America. Unfortunately, an armadillo can't take its armor off when it crosses a river. So it does the next best thing: it gulps down air until its stomach blows up like a balloon, then away it floats.

You'd be an excellent diver if you were as good at it as a moose. A moose can dive twice its own height or more to munch on plants growing on the bottom.

How would you keep cool in the summer if you had to wear a hot suit? A penquin's fancy suit un-fortunately is a warm one in summer. But a penquin keeps cool just the same by pumping extra blood into its thin-skinned feet and flippers. When it flaps its flippers, heat escapes from its body.

# Summer Log

There are so many things to see and do in summer, sometimes it's hard to remember them all. That's why we're giving you these charts to write and draw on. If you run out of room, you can make your own charts in a little notebook. That way you can carry them with you — and maybe even hand them in at the end of the summer as a school project.

**Signs of Summer or Fall**

| Date | Time | What I Saw |
|------|------|------------|
|      |      |            |
|      |      |            |
|      |      |            |
|      |      |            |
|      |      |            |

**Most Amazing Summer Days**

| Date | Time | What I Saw or Did |
|------|------|-------------------|
|      |      |                   |
|      |      |                   |
|      |      |                   |
|      |      |                   |
|      |      |                   |

**Interesting Tracks I've Seen**

| Date | Who Made Them | What They Looked Like |
|------|---------------|-----------------------|
|      |               |                       |
|      |               |                       |
|      |               |                       |
|      |               |                       |
|      |               |                       |

**Interesting Things I've Seen**

| Date | Time | What I Saw |
|------|------|------------|
|      |      |            |
|      |      |            |
|      |      |            |
|      |      |            |
|      |      |            |

## Most Amazing Summer Days

| Date | Time | What I Saw or Did |
|------|------|-------------------|
|      |      |                   |
|      |      |                   |
|      |      |                   |
|      |      |                   |
|      |      |                   |

## Signs of Summer or Fall

| Date | Time | What I Saw |
|------|------|------------|
|      |      |            |
|      |      |            |
|      |      |            |
|      |      |            |
|      |      |            |

## Interesting Things I've Seen

| Date | Time | What I Saw |
|------|------|------------|
|      |      |            |
|      |      |            |
|      |      |            |
|      |      |            |
|      |      |            |

## Interesting Tracks I've Seen

| Date | Who Made Them | What They Looked Like |
|------|---------------|-----------------------|
|      |               |                       |
|      |               |                       |
|      |               |                       |
|      |               |                       |
|      |               |                       |

# The Inside Story of a Wasps' Nest

Warning: *NEVER EXAMINE A WASPS' NEST, EXCEPT FROM A DISTANCE, IN SPRING, SUMMER OR FALL — YOU CAN GUESS WHAT MIGHT HAPPEN.*

**One winter, artist and naturalist Anker Odum found a wasps' nest in a hawthorn bush. As the temperature had been below freezing for months he knew the nest could not contain any living wasps. The only wasps to survive the winter are queens, and they hibernate away from their nest. He knew he could safely look in the nest and describe and draw what he saw. It was like trying to solve a mystery puzzle...**

When I carefully peeled off the outer covering on one side, I found that all the inhabitants were long dead, mummified — or rather, freeze-dried — from the long cold months. The only adult wasp left in the colony lay dead just inside the entrance hole. The others were all wasp grubs and pupae, and all still in their cells. Although it was small as wasps' nests go — about the size of my fist — it contained, as far as I could estimate, about 1,000 cells. The building was in four stories, and a stalk of grass went through the whole nest, connecting the floors like a fireman's sliding pole. Apparently this had grown after the start of the colony, and the wasps had simply built around it.

The cells were in two stages of development — some were open, octagonal cells, grey like the outside of the nest. These contained grubs. Other cells were closed with a whitish hood, like the finger of a white glove. Some of these hoods had been cut through, when their inhabitants emerged as adult wasps. Others were still intact, containing wasp pupae in various stages. One hood was almost cut through, a pair of antennae stuck out, and a black eye was visible inside. Its inhabitant had been overcome by the cold just as it was ready to begin life as an adult wasp.

From what I could see in the nest, and what I already knew about wasps, I could imagine how the colony had been made. The nest had been started by one lonely queen after she awoke from hibernation last spring and had been completed later by her offspring.

1. Cells are like small "rooms" in the nest where the young wasps live. These open cells contain the eggs and the young wasps (larvae) just hatched from the eggs. In this stage the larvae look like grubs and are fed by the adult wasps.

2. This wasps' nest has four stories.

3. Each floor is suspended by a strong paper stalk.

4. A grass stalk has grown through the nest.

5. The larvae have sealed themselves in these closed cells with a white silken hood. During this time they change into adult wasps.

6. A paper-like envelope covers the nest.

7. The opening or door to the nest.

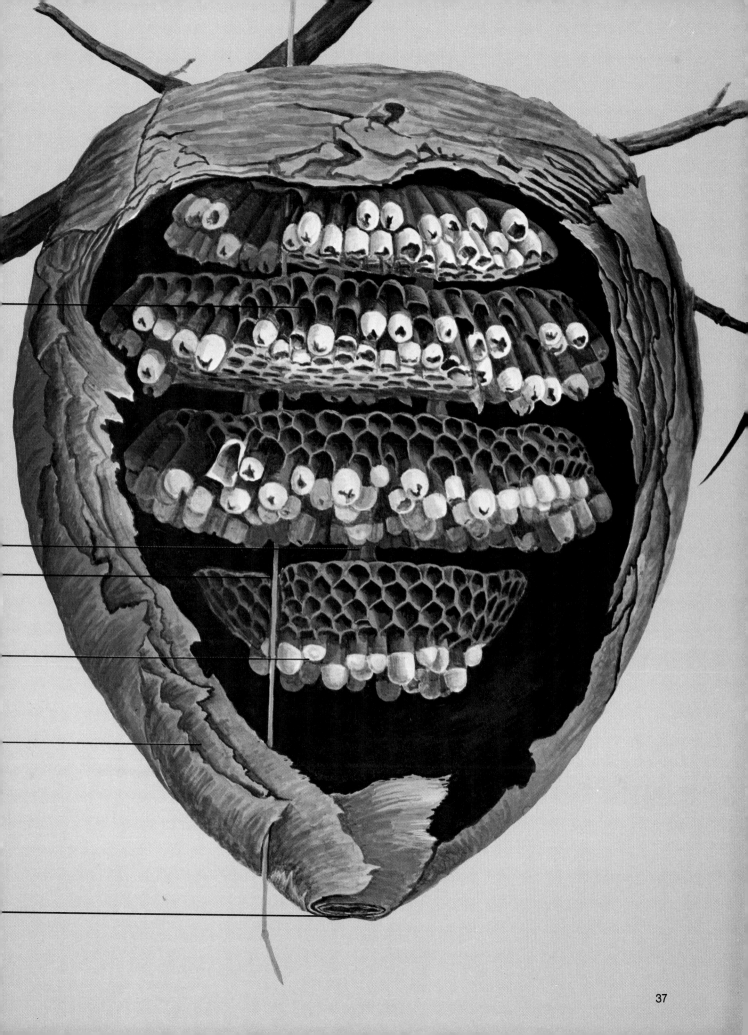

# How a Wasps' Nest is Built

1. After finding a nest-site, the queen wasp flies to the nearest dry old tree trunk or gate-post, where she shaves off wood fibers with her mandibles (jaws).

2. Carrying the fibers in a ball under her chin, she flies back to the site, wets the wood with fluid from her mouth, making paper pulp, and smears it onto the underside of the branch. Again and again she flies back for more.

3. From the smear she draws a short stalk downward, and on its end builds a small, upside down cup. This is the first cell of the colony.

## The Stages From Egg to Wasp

1. An empty cell.
2. An egg attached to the top of the cell.
3. In this cell you can see the egg after it has hatched into a grub or larva.
4. The grub has changed into a pupa, which is sealed in the cell by a white silken hood.
5. A new wasp cuts through the hood. It's wings and antennae are ready to unfold.
6. The empty cell left by the wasp.

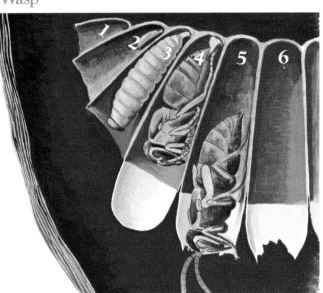

## A Close-up of the

1. A wasp larva in its cell. Its head is poking up as it waits to be fed.

4. As she adds more cells, the adjoining ones flatten the sides of the inner ones, making them octagonal. Now she builds a kind of umbrella over the cells. In the meantime she has laid eggs in the first cells, and while she works she also feeds the first new wasp grubs.

5. Soon the umbrella has expanded into a closed envelope which covers the whole nest. Several of the first grubs have already turned into pupae, and soon new adult worker wasps emerge to help the queen. They take over the work of building and feeding the grubs, while the queen retires from all duties but egg-laying.

## Changes from Larva to Wasp

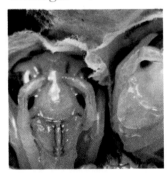

2. A close-up of the pupa with the silken hood removed.

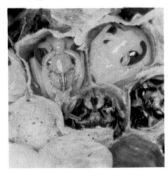

3. In this picture you can see five pupae. The two in the lower part of the picture have almost completed their transformation into adult wasps.

4. The adult wasp coming out of the cell in which it has lived as an egg, larva and pupa.

5. The wasp walking on a section of the cone.

39

# How to Be a Happy Hiker

Hiking is fast becoming one of the most popular sports — not just with the kids but everybody. With good reason — it's fun! But there's more to it than simply heading into the woods to seek adventure.

First a few basic rules. Getting lost *is* serious. In order *not to get lost* you should always hike on a specially marked trail, in a city park where there are people around, or with an adult.

Always tell someone exactly where you plan to go and how long you plan to be away.

*Never hike alone.*

Plan to be home before dark, but in case an accident delays you, carry a flashlight in your pack.

Short hikes are better than long hikes. Go slowly so you can see more, and remember that you'll be much more tired on the way back.

Wear several layers of light clothing rather than one layer of heavy clothing, so you can peel off one or two layers when it's hot. Long sleeves, pant legs and a brimmed hat give you better protection from sun, bugs, scratchy twigs, etc. Always pack rain gear too — just in case.

Always carry a whistle. Hang it around your neck and don't take it off (in case you lose it!). Never blow your whistle unless you are hurt or lost.

For a long hike, two pairs of socks are be than one. A thin pa next to your skin w help prevent blisters

A squirrel might enjoy your apple core — but don't leave any other litter.

You need a backpack to carry your gear. An old school bag will do or improvise with a plastic grocery bag.

Quiet hikers see more, so leave your city voice behind. Why not invent your own silent signals such as "a raised hand" to indicate stop, etc.

If you don't have a water canteen (and this is a most important piece of equipment) make one by tying a plastic bottle in an old sock — a vinegar bottle works well.

To record your discoveries, tie a note pad and blunt pencil to your belt. You can sketch tracks, etc. and look them up later in the library.

If you're planning to fish, carry your line and hook inside a 35 mm film can.

You'll use lots of energy hiking, so take high-energy foods with you. For lunch: sandwiches, cheese, raisins, boiled eggs, carrot and celery sticks, cookies and an apple. For snacks: "Gorp" a treat experienced hikers make by mixing some of the following in a plastic bag: shelled nuts, shelled sunflower seeds, chocolate chips, raisins, tiny marshmallows or jelly beans. Also carry an orange in case you run out of water and get thirsty.

A first-aid kit can be handy. Pack in it some adhesive bandages, disinfectant, cotton wool, insect repellent and toilet paper.

TRAIL

This is poison ivy. Avoid it.

41

is an imaginary hike. On a real hike, you can discover *some* of nature's wonders. See how many you can find in this maze by drawing a line from the start to the finish, touching as many sets of footprints as you can along the way without retracing your path.

**START**

# Summer Snacks

Some of these snacks take seconds to make, others a little longer, but they're all easy. And, you'll be pleased to know they're not only good, but every one is good for you, too. Dig in...

## Juice Cubes

Pour your favorite juice into an ice cube tray and place in the freezer. When the juice is frozen, you'll have juice cubes. Try putting lemonade cubes into orange juice! Mmmm. Mmmm.

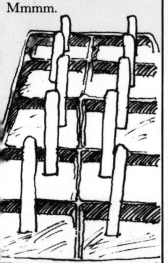

## Banana cooler

You'll need:
4 ripe bananas
small knife and cutting board
½ cup freshly squeezed lemon juice
1 cup vanilla ice cream
3 tablespoons honey
1 cup plain yogurt
electric blender
4 tall glasses
an adult to help you

1. Peel and slice the bananas and soak the slices in lemon juice for five minutes.
2. Put the bananas and lemon juice and all the other ingredients in the blender. Blend until smooth.
3. Pour into glasses and enjoy.

## Icy fruit

To make 2 or 3 glassfuls you'll need:
tray of ice cubes
small plastic bag
large bowl
rolling pin
wooden spoon, fork or potato masher
1 cup of juicy fruit (watermelon, pineapple, peach chunks, raspberries, strawberries, etc.)

1. Put the ice cubes in the plastic bag and make crushed ice by banging the bag with a rolling pin. (If the plastic bag is thin, put it inside a towel.)
2. Put the fruit in a large bowl and mash it with a wooden spoon, fork or potato masher.
3. Add the crushed ice and stir.
4. Spoon into glasses for a neat treat.

## Juicesicles

You'll need:
a can of your favorite frozen fruit juice concentrate
water
small bowl
paper cups
popsicle sticks

1. Mix your frozen juice with 1½ cans of water in a bowl.
2. Fill each cup with juice and put in the freezer.
3. After 45 minutes or so, check to see if ice crystals are forming in the juice. If so, stand, a popsicle stick in the middle of each cup. If not, try again in 5 or 10 minutes.
4. When the popsicles are frozen, peel away the paper cups.

### Frozen banana

Toss a whole peeled banana in the freezer. Once it's frozen, you'll have one cool treat.

### Fruited honey treats

Dip your favorite fruit (peach chunks, apple chunks, strawberries, grapes) into just enough honey to coat the fruit, then place in a large glass or plastic container with a lid. Screw on the lid, give the jar a shake and store in the refrigerator for a sweet treat.

### Mini grapesicles

Wrap loose, washed seedless grapes in foil and put them in the freezer. After three hours, take them out and pop them into your mouth for a cool surprise.

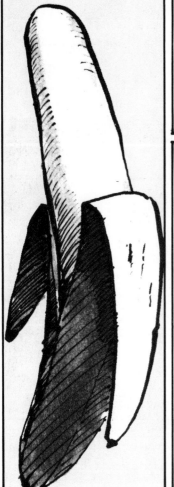

### Banana ice cream

You'll need:
electric blender
wooden spoon
10 marshmallows
2 bananas
1/3 cup milk
2 tablespoons sugar
1 teaspoon lemon juice
1 cup heavy cream
mixing bowl (not plastic as the cream won't whip!)
ice tray
an adult to help you

1. Put everything except the heavy cream into an electric blender and mix on high speed.
2. In a bowl whip the cream until it makes peaks that stand up like mountain peaks.
3. Slowly add the blended mixture to the whipped cream. Pour it into an ice tray (you might need two) and put it into the freezer until frozen.

### A triple yummy

Make a triple decker cookie/jam/ice cream sandwich. It tastes even better when it's been in the freezer for an hour.

## Banana goop refrigerator pie

You'll need:

1 cup graham cracker crumbs (about 12 to 14 graham wafers)
¼ cup melted butter
2 tablespoons honey
bowl
aluminum pie plate at least 23 cm/9 in. wide
1 cup hot water
1 tablespoon unflavored gelatin (one envelope)
electric blender
¼ cup oil
1 egg
1 teaspoon vanilla
3 bananas

1. Make a crust by stirring the graham cracker crumbs, melted butter and honey in a bowl with your fingers or a fork. Press the crust into a pie plate, making sure you don't leave holes.
2. To make the filling put the water and gelatin in a blender and blend until the gelatin is dissolved.
3. Add the oil, egg, vanilla and bananas and blend until smooth.
4. Pour this mixture into your pie plate and pop in the refrigerator for several hours.

Instead of the banana goop, you might want to fill the pie shell with your favorite flavor of ice cream, softened a little so you can spread it. Then put it in a freezer until solid.

## Yopsicles

Mash up your favorite fruit and add it to plain yogurt and pour the mixture into paper cups. Put a popsicle stick into each one and pop them in the freezer for at least two hours. To get at your yopsicle, dip the cup quickly into warm water and it will slide right off. If your yopsicle is too mouth-puckering, add a bit of honey.

## Make any drink cooler...

Here's an easy way to make any drink cooler. Dip the rim of your glass in your favorite fruit juice and then into white sugar. Stash the glass in the freezer for a couple of minutes. Take it out and fill-er-up with your favorite cold drink.

# Lights Over Loon Lake

## A science fiction story by Monica Hughes

The color drained out of the sky and twilight settled softly over the still waters of Loon Lake.

"It's beautiful," Elaine whispered. She and Chris were drinking their before-bed cup of hot chocolate, sitting on the rocky headland of the island. They could see the whole western end of the lake and the low Gatineau Hills beyond.

"Why are you whispering?" Chris asked in an ordinary voice, which sounded almost like shouting.

"Shhh! I'm listening to the quiet."

Chris listened too. There was the soft sound of water lapping at the edges of their island. There was a sudden popping sound, which must have been resin exploding inside the firewood back at their camp. Then there were only the sounds of the water again.

The stars began to come out in ones and twos, and soon, as if encouraged by the others, in whole groups and patterns, until the sky was full of them.

"After the city," Elaine said softly, "I didn't know places could be this quiet."

A sudden, shivering cry ran across the surface of the lake. It was followed by an inhuman laugh that echoed crazily around the dark hills. Both children jumped to their feet. Afterward Chris said that it was Elaine who clutched at him, but *she* said that he was holding on to her just as hard.

"A monster! It's a monster. Oh, let's go back to Mom and Dad."

"It can't be." Chris's teeth were chattering. "There aren't such things nowadays. You know that." He stared out over the dark water. A darker shape bobbed on the surface and as suddenly vanished. He laughed with relief. "Loons, that's all. A couple of old loons diving and calling."

"Are you sure? They sounded so spooky. Not a bit the way they are on TV."

"Of course I'm sure. It's just so dark and quiet, that's all. Oh darn, I've spilled my chocolate."

"Have the rest of mine."

"Halves, okay?"

They sat and sipped in turn, looking out into the darkness, hoping for another glimpse of the birds.

"Chris, what's that? Oh, look!"

"Is it the loons? Where? Oh!" Chris stopped talking suddenly and stared across the lake with his mouth open. Along the north shore, above the beach, danced two shimmering blobs of strange, greenish light.

"What do you think it is?"

"I don't know. I've never... that green is weird, isn't it? Like northern lights."

"But whoever heard of northern lights moving around in blobs like enormous flashlights, and floating...oh, Chris, look at that!"

*That* was the lights joining each other in midair above the trees, as if in conversation. They separated again and sank to treetop level, like ghostly figures in a dance, to bob along the shore, one to the east and the other to the west.

"Almost as if they were looking for something," Elaine guessed.

"Kids!" It was Dad's voice, comfortably ordinary, shouting from the campsite. "Time for bed. Come on!"

"Now we"ll *never* know what the spooky lights really were," Chris grumbled as they hurried along the twisted path; but Elaine felt that she'd seen more than enough for one night. There was something very comforting about the glow of the fire on the tents, and about wriggling down into a warm sleeping bag with nothing left out except the tip of a nose and the top of a head.

Next morning, in ordinary sunlight, with the smell of bacon and woodsmoke, and the chatter of squirrels and birds, Elaine began to feel quite brave again.

When Dad said, "I don't know if you kids have any plans, but I'm going fishing. Do you want to come too?" she looked meaningfully at Chris.

"May we please take one of the canoes across to the north shore and explore a bit by ourselves? We'll be very careful."

Mother and Father looked at each other, "Well..."

"You know we're safe in canoes," Chris added. "We had all that training at the Y. And we won't forget our life jackets for an instant. Honest!"

"Suppose you were to get lost?"

"Oh, Mom, how could we? You can see the lake and our campsite from everywhere. And if Dad's out there fishing, he'll be able to see us too, won't he?"

"Well..."

"I'll start making sandwiches right away," said Elaine. "So don't expect us back for lunch."

"You mustn't drink any water from the lake or streams," Mother said, relenting. "I'll make you a canteen of boiled water and you'll have to make that last."

Quickly, in case the parents should change their minds, Chris and Elaine stowed a small backpack containing cheese-and-tomato sandwiches, oranges, the water and a small first-aid kit—just in case—in the bottom of the canoe. Chris had wanted to take the map and a compass, but Dad said that was ridiculous.

"I don't want you to get the idea that you're world explorers. Stick to the nearby shoreline."

Chris steered the canoe toward the place where they had first seen the green lights. They passed the loons bobbing on the water like large, dark ducks, but now they didn't even turn to watch where the birds came up after their dives. Their eyes were on the shore, searching for clues.

The beach was sloping and sandy, and Elaine hopped neatly out without even getting her sneakers wet, then held the bow steady for Chris. Then they lifted the canoe right out of the water and turned it over.

"You never know," Chris said, when Elaine begged him to hurry up. "Remember Dad's story about when he was a boy and they opened up a dam to let the logs go down, and when he came back his canoe was floating down the lake all by itself."

"At least we've got Dad for a lookout. He'd see if anything went wrong." Elaine hopped from foot to foot with excitement. "Oh, do come on!"

Chris stowed their life jackets and the paddles neatly under the overturned canoe. "There. Now, which way first?" He looked along the beach. "Or do you suppose we should separate?"

"Let's not. It's more fun together. Besides, suppose one of us were to meet a wild animal?"

They walked west along the shore. There were no wild animals. In fact there were no footprints at all in smooth sand, except for the tiny, fan-shaped feet of sandpipers and the trail of their own sneakers. The shore was littered with driftwood and old whitened logs.

"We can make a great fire."

"Later maybe. It's far too hot now."

It *was* hot, and getting steadily hotter. There was no shade at all down on the beach and the sun beat down on their heads out of a cloudless sky. Elaine stopped. "I'm so thirsty."

"You can't be yet. We just got here."

"I am. My lips are getting all cracked."

"If we start drinking now it'll never last."

"Just a tiny sip. Please, Chris."

But the tiny sip made her feel even hotter. There was nothing to see on the beach, and when they came to a place where water trickled down between pebbles, they turned thankfully away from the dazzle of hot sand and followed the trickle up into the coolness of the trees. Over many years the little stream had worn a deep furrow through the soil, and now grass and small bushes and saplings grew on either side, joining together above it to make a cool, damp, green tunnel.

Elaine bent down to the water.

"Don't drink it, silly!" Chris called out sharply.

"I'm not. Just wetting my face. Try it. It feels wonderful."

Chris bent down. As his hands touched the cool water, his eyes were on the level of the bank just ahead. He stared, forgot about being hot and straightened up again.

"What is it?"

"Footprints, I think. But funny. Not like anything I've seen, even in pictures."

"Not bears? Or maybe a moose? Oh, Chris, maybe we'd better go back to the beach. I'd hate to meet something coming at me in here."

"Come and look, silly billy. They're nothing like a bear's or a moose's either. Nothing like any kind of animal."

"You mean they're people's? Phooey! I thought this was such a secret place there'd be nobody here but us."

"Just look," was all Chris would say, and when Elaine had scrambled over some stones to where Chris was standing she could see that indeed the footprints couldn't belong to a person. They were too narrow for a start, and they were tiny, not much bigger than a baby's foot. When she bent down to look at them closely, she could see that there were no toe marks either.

"Why, they *are* shoe prints!" she exclaimed. "Baby shoe prints."

"They can't be. Whoever has shoes *that* shape?"

"Look for yourself. There's even a design on the bottom."

"You mean like Adidas or North Star? There can't be!"

"There it is, large as life. Oh, don't you understand, Chris? These are people prints, but not human people!"

"Not...?"

"The lights were unearthly too, weren't they? The same kind of thing."

"You mean... little green men and flying saucers and all that sort of thing?" Chris let out his breath in a whistle and then ran his hand through his hair until it stood wildly up on end. "We could follow them and find out. It'd be fun, wouldn't it?" His voice wasn't very convincing.

"I'm scared, Chris. I don't think I want to."

Elaine's scaredness made Chris feel a whole lot braver. "Oh, come on. It was *you* who had the idea of finding out about the green lights. The footprints must be a part of it."

"I know. That's why I'm scared. Suppose we meet someone 10 feet tall with horrible buggy eyes and...and a ray gun?"

"Oh, come on, we won't. After all, these footprints are tiny, not much bigger than a hare's." Chris caught Elaine's hand and pulled her along with him, upstream through the green tunnel of shadowy trees and bushes.

Elaine's heart was beating so loudly that she was sure Chris could hear it, and she kept expecting an enormous *something* to burst out of the tangle of brush just ahead of them, in spite of the evidence of the tiny shoe prints. It was with a mixed feeling of relief and disappointment that they at last came out of the leafy tunnel onto high, rocky ground, into ordinary bright sunshine, and without a single footprint to show them which way to go.

"Darn it!" Chris stopped and peered at the ground. "It's as dry as a bone up here. Which way should we go, I wonder?"

"Let's not. Perhaps we've gone far enough."

"Fiddle! Look, you can see Dad down there on the lake, fishing away like mad."

Elaine turned and looked. Sure enough, there was Dad lying comfortably in the canoe, his shoulders against the stern thwart. His line was in the water. She couldn't see his face because his hat was over it, but she could bet that his eyes were shut. She looked across at their campsite. There was Mother's bright red shirt on the rocky lookout. She was sitting down, reading a book or writing letters, Elaine thought. She smiled and felt much better. It was such a nice, ordinary day that nothing very peculiar could happen, could it?

"All right," she said bravely. "Why don't we go on following the stream? It must go somewhere."

It led them along a twisting, stoney path between two bald, rocky hills, and then suddenly vanished into a crack between two boulders.

"That's it then." Chris looked around.

"And we can't see the lake any more. Suppose we got lost?"

"We can't possibly. All we have to do is to follow the stream downhill again. Let's have lunch while we work out what to do next. I'm starving."

He looked around for some shade. The sun shimmered on the rocks and the air quivered with heat. There were no trees up here, but there *was* a shadow in the glare of the southern slope.

"Over there, Elaine. But be careful. You could easily twist your ankle on all those loose rocks."

They found that the shadow was a cave, cool and dark and dusty. They sat in the opening — neither of them felt comfortable about actually going *inside* — and shared the sandwiches and oranges and drinks of water, now very warm. Chris was just screwing the top back on the canteen when a low moaning sound shivered out of the darkness behind them. Elaine screamed. Chris dropped the canteen and jumped to his feet.

"What was *that*?"

"In the cave! Oh, Chris, it came from inside the cave."

"I wish we had a flashlight with us."

"We've got matches. But maybe we'd better not. Maybe we'd better go away." Elaine was outside in the comfortable sunshine when the sound came again. She hesitated, and then went back and hunted through the backpack until she'd found the matches.

"No, Elaine. You were right. We'd better go."

"It's not angry. You can tell by the sound. It's hurting."

"Hurt animals can be really dangerous. Come on. We'll go and tell Dad. He'll know what to do."

"We just can't go away and leave it." Elaine wasn't really listening to him. Her teeth were chattering and her fingers shook so that the first match went out. She screwed the paper bag their sandwiches had been in into a tight stick and lit the end. She held it up and peered into the darkness.

The cave was deeper than she'd imagined it would be. She had to walk slowly forward into the

shadows until the flames flickered off the back wall and she could see, they could both see, the small figure on the floor at the very back. It was like a fish, she thought, a silvery fish with arms and legs, a shining fish that moaned piteously and seemed to be trying to tell them something.

The twisted paper bag burned down to Elaine's fingers. "Ow!" She dropped it and put her fingers in her mouth. The dark was now much blacker than it had been before. She fumbled for another match.

"No, don't." Chris caught her wrist. "Wait a minute. Our eyes will adapt. It's just the sun made it seem so dark."

He was right. Slowly the blackness turned to a grey with shadows in it. It was terrifying waiting, wondering what they were going to see. Neither of them spoke. There was only a faint whimper from the shadowy thing on the floor of the cave.

As soon as she could see properly, Elaine knelt down and timidly put out her hand. Touching it was scary at first. She had thought it might be slimy, like a fish, but it wasn't at all. The silveriness was only a kind of cloth that covered the creature completely except for its face and hands. Once she had touched it she wasn't afraid any more, but ran her hands carefully over its body. When she touched its left ankle it cried out and tried to move away.

"Oh, I'm sorry I hurt you. Chris, look. Can you tell if it's broken?"

"I don't know. Isn't it tiny? But it looks awfully swollen next to the other. I'll see if I can find some straight sticks down in the bush to make splints. We'll bind it up before we try to move it."

When Chris got back, Elaine held the foot as gently as she could while Chris tied it up with bandages out of the first-aid kit.

"Its leg feels so cold, Chris. Like ice!"

"Perhaps it's in shock. And it's really chilly back here. I think we ought to get it into the sun, where it's warm."

"Do you think we *should* move it?"

"We'll have to risk it. Suppose it died of cold? We'll go really slowly, Elaine. You on one side and me on the other."

They lifted the creature out into the sunlight. It moaned when they first moved it, then went limp.

"Oh, my goodness!" Elaine stared. The creature was almost her height, but as thin as a twig, with the ugliest face she had ever seen. Its nose was flat against its cheeks, its mouth a wide, lipless oblong. It was as pale as its silver suit and its slitty eyes were closed.

There was just a little water left in the bottle, which, luckily being plastic, had bounced instead of breaking when Chris had dropped it. Elaine soaked a

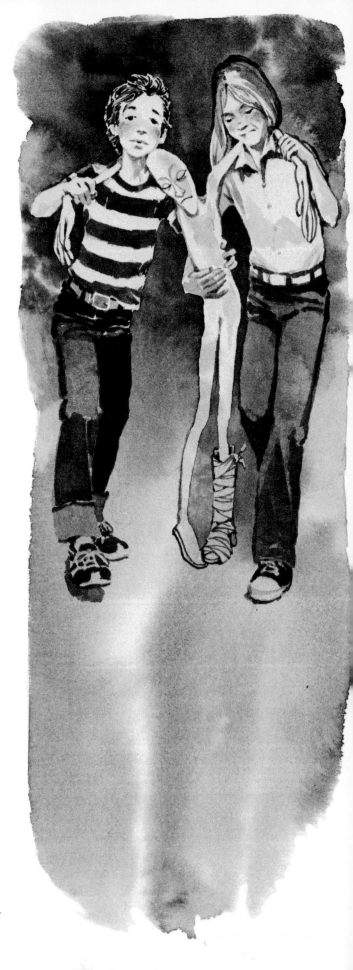

pad out of the first-aid kit and gently washed the dust off the ugly little face. The eyelids, as hairless as a lizard's, suddenly opened, and a narrow, pointed purple tongue flickered out of the lipless mouth.

"Oh, it's coming alive again!" She couldn't help drawing back a little. It was so very ugly.

The yellow eyes stared past them at the sun, and, as clearly as if it were written in them, Elaine saw fear and despair. The little creature struggled to sit up, wincing at the pain. Then its eyes shut, its mouth made a square and it began to cry, large tears jumping from its eyes and running down its flat, pale cheeks.

Elaine forgot to be afraid. "Why, you're only a baby!" She put her arms around it. "Please don't cry. It'll be all right. We'll help." She rocked it gently until the wails became hiccups and the tears stopped. 'What's the matter? Where have you come from? Who are you? Oh, I wish you could tell us!"

Almost as if it understood — but how could it? — the silver child pointed up at the sky, and then, with a finger as thin as a drinking straw, began to draw in the dirt at the edge of the cave. It drew circles and star shapes, and with a curved fingernail lightly skimmed a path between them.

"You're from out there? From another planet?" Elaine knew she should be surprised — even not believe it — but once having seen the silver child, where on earth could it come from, except *not* from earth? "I'm Elaine and this is my brother Chris. Who are you?" She put her hand gently on its chest, and it responded with a clicking snort that she couldn't begin to imitate. "I'm going to call you Starchild," she told it, and the creature smiled — at least the enormous mouth widened as if it understood.

"Poor thing," Elaine said.

"This is crazy," Chris spluttered. "It can't really be happening. There aren't such things as people from outer space. It's been *proved*."

"Starchild's right here, isn't he? And he's hurt and dreadfully scared."

"The way you're clutching him, I'm not surprised."

"He is not afraid of me. Look." Sure enough, Starchild gave a last shuddering sniff and snuggled closer. "It was seeing the sun that scared him so. Why? Do you suppose they're night creatures?"

Starchild stirred. The twig-like arm shot out and again drew in the dust. A circle. He patted the ground. A star shape. He pointed up at the sun, now well into the afternoon. He traced a circle round the circle and held up one finger.

"That's earth," Elaine said, suddenly understanding. "Turning once on itself is a day. What is

going to happen in a day, Starchild? No, don't cry again. We'll help. Only tell us."

A skinny hand brushed across the dirt and the fingers drew again. Not a circle this time, but a squashed shape, rather like a lemon, with things sticking out of it. They both stared.

"Oh, no. It doesn't look like anything. Is it supposed to be an animal? Ow, don't....!" She winced and put her hand to her head.

"What's the matter?"

"When he shouted like that my head hurt dreadfully."

"He didn't shout. He didn't make a sound." Chris stared. "Elaine, are you all right?"

"I think so. The pain's gone. Why didn't you hear it? It was an awful noise, as if he were angry."

"Perhaps it was telepathy. Inside your head, you know. Only he doesn't know how to do it properly."

"That's a terrific idea." Elaine put both her arms around Starchild and tried to make her own thoughts calm and soothing, instead of scared to death and full of frantic questions. At first it didn't seem to work, but after a while all kinds of strange pictures began to flit into her mind, things she would never have thought of by herself. She saw cliffs, high and blue, with tall, willowy trees of purple and grey, and huge birds with tail feathers streaming every color of the rainbow. And big people, as ugly as Starchild, but in some way very special and dear....

"Oh, my goodness!" Elaine's voice was sharp with horror.

"What is it?"

"He and his parents came to earth on a ship, for repairs, I think. And they have to leave at sunset. I mean, they *have* to go, whether they find Starchild or not. Our sun and moon and planets have to be in just the right places in the sky for them to take off, and that's at sunset *today*!"

"Does he know where the ship is?"

As soon as Chris spoke, Starchild turned in Elaine's arms and pointed down at the tangle of green that lay below them to the north.

"We'll *never* find them in that. We'd better get Dad. He'll know what to do."

"There's not enough time, Chris. It can't be too far away. He's too little to have come far by himself. I wonder how he got separated from his parents? You'd think they'd be more careful on a strange planet, wouldn't you?"

As soon as she spoke, Elaine felt that she was watching a picture inside her mind, a bit like television, but at the same time she *was* the person in the picture and could feel *his* feelings.

She saw two tall figures working over some

53

machinery. She saw Starchild looking longingly out of the spaceship door at the green forest. She could feel how bored he was, with nothing to do but wait. A rabbit hip-hopped past the ship and disappeared between the trees.

"Oh, what's that?" Starchild could bear it no longer. He slid out of the door and followed the brown hopper through the trees and up the hill, never noticing where the rabbit was leading him.

Then came a sudden tumble among the rocks. a waking up to pain. Crawling up the green tunnel to the bare hill top. Tired. Frightened. Hurting. The cave was not as scary, it was a bit like the spaceship home. Falling asleep inside the cave. Waking up to a new day. Alone....

Starchild's eyes screwed up and the tears began to run down his cheeks again.

"Oh, don't cry! We'll find your parents in time, won't we, Chris?"

"I hope so." Chris looked gloomily down at the crumpled green mass of trees and hills and valleys. It seemed to go on for ever. "If we don't find the right place and get back to Loon Lake before sunset he won't be the only one who's lost, you know!"

"But we have to try, Chris. We can't *not* try!"

"Oh, I know. How'll we get him down there, with his ankles busted?"

"Piggyback, I guess. If you carry him, I'll go ahead and try and pick the easiest way down."

They started down the hill, with Starchild on Chris's shoulders and Elaine in front, so that Chris could keep his balance against her shoulder in the steepest places. They toiled up the next hill. It was trees all the way, heavy going, and by the time they got to the top Chris's knees were buckling.

Elaine took Starchild on her back. He was far heavier than she'd expected, and to make it worse, his fear was sending jabs of pain into her head. Down into the next valley she carried him, staggering against Chris, against tree trunks.

I can't, she thought. But I must, she told her tired body. Some instinct — or was it Starchild leading her? — made her turn to the west, along a twisting valley. It was awfully hot, and the mosquitoes were driving her frantic.

There was a glimmer ahead. Another lake? Elaine's heart sank. If it were a lake they'd have to find a way around it. And she couldn't. She simply couldn't....

Now the glimmer was close by. Now it was directly ahead of them. Starchild's arms tightened around her neck so that she choked and stumbled. They they were out of the trees and into a small clearing, and it was right there in front of them,

silver, glowing, wonderful and quite unbelievable — a flying saucer!

Starchild cried out, and an opening appeared in the curved silver wall. A figure strode towards them, huge, much taller than Father, but as thin as an aspen. Elaine wanted to run, but she couldn't drop poor Starchild, so she stood quite still with her eyes tightly shut.

The weight was lifted from her shoulders and then a hand touched her cheek. She opened her eyes. Why had she thought them ugly? They were beautiful in their happiness. It shone out past the strange, lashless eyes, the oblong, lipless mouth.

A second tall one appeared, running through the trees, and Elaine could feel his joy too. He put his hands on Elaine's and Chris's shoulders, gently, as if saying thank you, and then they both went back into their ship carrying the dear, ugly little Starchild. When the door closed you couldn't see that there had ever been a door.

Elaine and Chris stood there and stared. Then a jay screamed nearby and Chris started. "Yipes! We'd better hurry if we're to get back before sunset."

"I don't want to..."

"We must!" He caught Elaine's hand and together they ran. Magically, their tiredness and hotness seemed to have left them. They didn't lose their way once. When they got back to the rocky hill and picked up their backpack from in front of the cave, there was Loon Lake lying below them as still as a piece of glass. Dad was just paddling his canoe back to the island. They couldn't see Mother, but a thread of smoke rose from the campsite.

"Come on! It'll be supper soon, and I'm starved!"

They didn't have much to say about their day ashore.

"Sounds pretty dull. Tomorrow you'd better come fishing with me," Dad remarked.

As soon as supper was over they went to the rocky lookout. The sun had set and color flooded the sky. The loons laughed crazily from across the crimson water. Low in the west the evening star appeared.

"There." Elaine pointed to the north shore.

A silent shape gleamed above the low hills. It rose, hovered, and then shot up and out of sight into the darkening sky.

"Right on time," said Chris with satisfaction.

"Goodbye, Starchild," Elaine whispered, and felt the happiness of the little stranger warm inside her.

# The Best Little Garden Ever

Somehow, vegetables taste even better when you've grown them youself. We won't fool you by saying gardening is easy; once you've planted seeds you are responsible for looking after them. But, if you don't try too much at once, you'll discover that gardening is fun as well as rewarding.

If you don't have a garden but only a balcony you can still grow radishes, potatoes and tomatoes in containers.

Container gardeners need:
large pots (or bushel baskets lined with plastic garbage bags with holes poked in the bottom)
small stones at the bottom of each pot or plastic bag for drainage
potting soil
a tray under each pot to catch any excess water.

If you do have room in a back yard, vegetables like pumpkins are great to try. All vegetables need lots of sun and water. Good luck!

### Perfect Potatoes

Potato plants grow very quickly and have lots of leaves and white flowers. To grow them, you'll need a potato with "eyes" that have started to sprout.
1. Cut the potatoes into large pieces, each piece having at least one but no more than three eyes.
2. Plant these sprouted eyes 10 cm/4 in. deep and 30 cm/12 in. apart in a pot outside or in a garden once there is no danger of frost.
When your plants are 30 cm/12 in. or taller they will begin to bloom. The plants will stop growing when their white petals drop. After several more weeks the leaves will yellow and fall. Now is the time to dig up your plants and see what you've got.

56

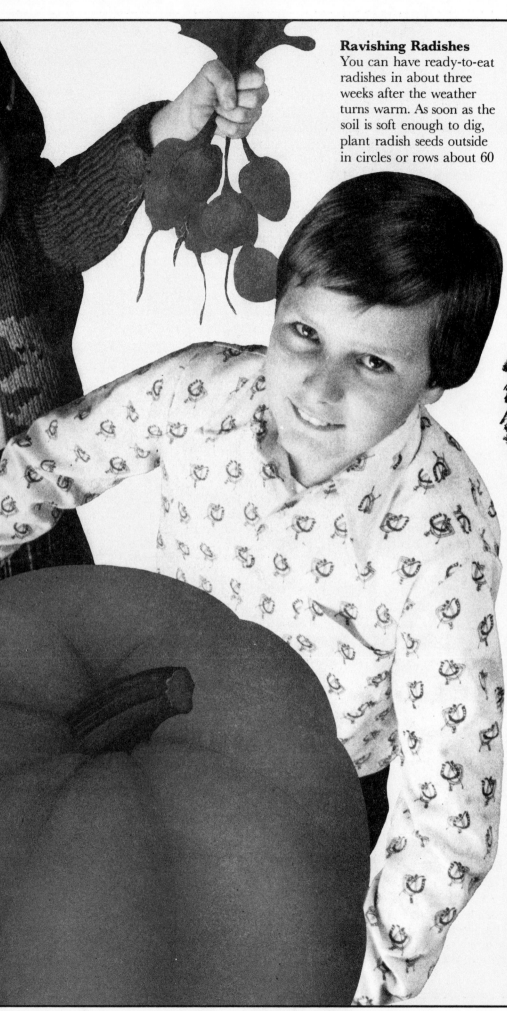

## Ravishing Radishes

You can have ready-to-eat radishes in about three weeks after the weather turns warm. As soon as the soil is soft enough to dig, plant radish seeds outside in circles or rows about 60 mm/2 in. apart and cover them lightly with earth. Thin them when they're about 2.5 cm/1 in. high. Keep the soil damp.

## Plump Pumpkins

You can watch pumpkins get bigger and fatter every day. Begin by mounding up the earth into a hill about 2 m/6 ft. in diameter and 10 cm/4 in. high.

1. Plant the seeds 1 cm/.4 in. deep, six to a mound, once there is no frost danger.
2. Keep the soil moist.
3. Seed leaves look like this:

4. When the plants begin to vine, pull out three or four of the smallest vines from the mound. If your vines grow longer with no signs of buds or blossoms, pinch back the tips of the vines.

Your pumpkin will have male and female flowers. The female flowers are the ones that turn into pumpkins, but only if they are fertilized by pollen from male flowers. Bees usually transfer this pollen, but if they don't visit your plants, you can do their job. Break off a male flower and gently rub its pollen-covered stamen into the center of the female flower.

A hint for larger pumpkins: break off all but one or two female flowers and all flowerless vines so more strength goes into forming the remaining flowers into pumpkins. Your pumpkin is ripe when it turns orange and the skin is hard.

# Tomato Plants

## Starting tomato plants indoors

To have home-grown tomatoes by midsummer start your seeds indoors in April. "Tiny Tim" seeds produce small cherry tomatoes, while "Bonny Best" or "Patio" make for larger tomatoes.

In addition to a large garden container you will need:
a foil cake pan with holes punched in the bottom
a piece of newspaper
a pencil
a few small and larger tin cans with holes in the bottom for planters

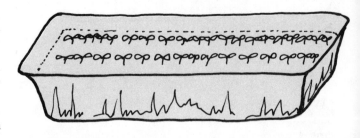

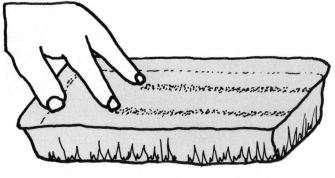

1. Fill the cake pan with moist potting soil. Make two rows (no more than 1 cm/.4 in. deep) in the soil by spreading two of your fingers 5 cm/2 in. apart and dragging them across the earth.

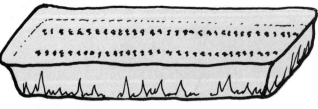

2. Sprinkle the seeds 1 cm/.4 in. apart in the rows. Do not cover them with soil.

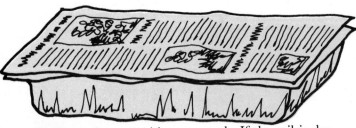

3. Cover the pan with a sheet of newspaper. Check your seeds daily and remove any moldy seeds. If the soil is dry, water with a gentle spray.

4. Remove the newspaper once the tiny leaves unfold. Place the container in a sunny window and keep the soil moist for a day or two.

5. When the seed leaves look hardy, transplant the seedlings into small tins. To do this, gently pry the seedlings out of the moist soil with a pencil.

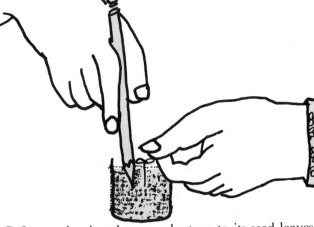

6. Before replanting the seedlings, nip .5 cm/.2 in. off the bottom of their roots to stimulate root growth. Then bury each plant up to its seed leaves in the soil in order to develop side roots and keep your plant sturdy.

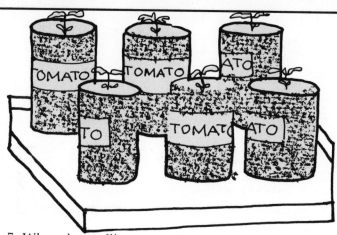

7. When the seedlings are about 5 cm/2 in. transplant them again into larger tin cans or similar containers. Nip their root tips off and plant the seedlings 3 cm/1 in. deeper than they were before to encourage root growth. Keep your plants in a sunny window and keep the soil moist. Always water seedlings with lukewarm water.

**Transplanting Tomatoes**
You should wait until at least mid-May when there is no chance of cold nights to transplant your tomatoes to the garden or a large outdoors pot.

In addition to your usual garden tools you will need:
a stake for each plant
some twine or strips of cloth
a toilet paper roll for each plant

2. Drive the stakes in first, then place your plant deep in the ground to encourage side root development.

3. Water the plants early in the day. Be careful not to get water on the leaves and stems.

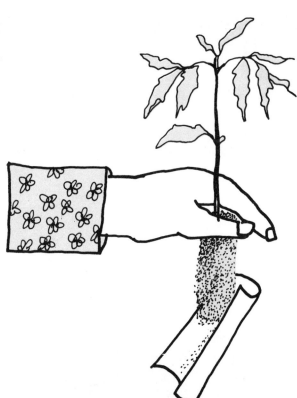

1. Remove the plants carefully from their pots and wrap toilet paper rolls around the roots and up to the first leaf. This will fend off cutworms until their season is over. By that time the paper should rot away.

4. As your plants grow, tie them to the stakes for support. In hot weather, tomato leaves may curl or get black spots from intense heat and lack of water. You shouldn't have a problem if you water your plants enough.

59

**Ho! Ho! Ho!**

Q. How do little fish make a living?
A. They start on a very small scale.

Q. How did the firefly feel when it ran into a fan?
A. Delighted.

Q. What game do judges play well?
A. Tennis — because it's played in court.

Q. Why is an elephant grey?
A. So you won't mistake him for a bluebird.

Q. When is a gardener like a mystery writer?
A. When he digs up plots.

I DARESAY THAT'S CLEVER!

Q. Why do elephants hide behind trees?
A. To trip ants.

Q. What would you serve but never want to eat?
A. A tennis ball.

Q. What do you get if you cross a sheep dog with a daisy?
A. Collie flowers.

Q. What do you call a cow eating grass?
A. A lawn mooer.

Q. Why does the ocean roar?
A. You would too if you had lobsters in your bed.

Q. Why are movie stars such cool people?
A. Because they have so many fans.

Q. Why was the florist suspicious of the flowers?
A. Because they were dis-covered in a garden plot.

Q. What's grey, has two ears, four legs and a trunk?
A. A mouse going on vacation.

# Keeping Cool

Ling-Ling has found the best spot in the Washington National Zoo to beat the heat. Because wild pandas live in faraway parts of China we don't know much about how they behave in their natural surroundings. But we do know that, like most animals, they feel uncomfortable in hot weather. What do they do when they can't jump in a tub?

Turn the page to find out...

Cats swim
. . . and so do birds.

**Hippos go wading**

**. . . while cows pause under a tree.**

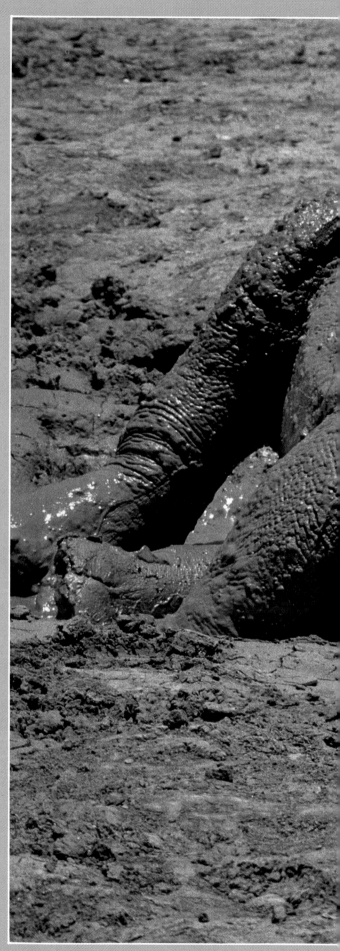

Lions take naps.
Marmots tunnel in the cool earth
. . . and big, fat rhinos wade in the squishy, squashy mud.

Penguins flap their flippers.
Sheep wear thick coats that
keep them surprisingly cool.
Dogs pant to pump out warm air
. . . and, like most mammals, so
does a bear.

# How You Can Keep Cool

If you haven't a boat to ride and you've already run through the hose five times this week, here's another great way to whoosh your way through summer — a backyard water slide. All you need is a thick plastic sheet, 10 m/ 32 ft. or so long which you can buy from a hardware store, and a soft, grassy slope. Smooth out the plastic and anchor it down at the sides with large stones. Jump into your bathing suit, turn the hose onto the plastic and away you go.

Be sure to check the ground carefully before you set up your slide to make sure there are no bumps, stones or sticks that could hurt your back or tear the plastic.

And remember to fold your slide up each night to give the grass underneath a chance to recover.

Need more ways to keep cool? Keep reading...

## Fan-dango

Fan-dango is a dance, but it sounds like it should be a good name for a fan, too. To make one, accordian fold a sheet of paper. Fold over one end for a handle, spread the folds gently apart and swoosh away. Instant air conditioning.

## Throw and Squirt

Balloon-a-splat! — All you do is fill some balloons with water and toss 'em around. If you're lucky one'll break as you catch it.

If you've got a few sponges handy you're ready for a sponge war. Soak them in a big bucket of water and fire away.

## Dress cool

Light-weight, light-colored, loose-fitting cotton clothes are cool summer wear for several cooling reasons: light colors reflect the sun away from your body; cotton absorbs perspiration and dries quickly; loose clothes act like a portable tent by not only keeping the sun's heat away from your body but also by letting in any cooling breezes. If you add sandals to your outfit instead of shoes, you'll be even cooler. Open shoes let the breezes circulate around your toes.

## Make a hot head hat

An old newspaper can be a super shady hat. Here's how:

1. Fold one sheet of newspaper like this:

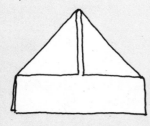

2. Fold the top corners so they meet.

3. Fold one of the bottom flaps in half like this:

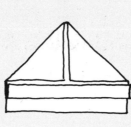

4. Then fold it up again like this:

5. Do the same for the other side.

Nick, Sophie and Mark Mite are three special kids with a big secret: they have discovered a way to shrink to any size they want and grow big again. If they shrink small enough they can float on air, even stay underwater for as long as they wish. It's a fine, summer day and the Mites are exploring a pond when they unexpectedly fall through a trapdoor into a world of miraculous creatures and sudden danger...

by Emily Hearn and Mark Thurman

# The Early Bird Earthworm Maze

finish

start

See if you can help the earthworm in the middle of this maze reach the surface safely by drawing a path to the flower garden. If you meet an ants' nest or another enemy of the earthworm such as the mole, the centipede or the carnivorous slug Testacella you must retrace your path. Also watch out for hungry birds!

# How to Be a Beach Detective

These children are beach detectives, and you can be one too, simply by turning the page. There you'll find two beach scenes, one at the ocean, the other at a lake or stream...

Rate yourself as a beach detective by seeing how many of the objects in these two beach scenes you can match up with the clues below. Write the numbers or letters opposite the clues. All the things on page 80 can be found on an ocean beach and all the things on page 81 can be found on an inland beach.
*Answers on page 128*

## Ocean Beach

☐ The skeleton of a sand dollar. A flat, round disk with five radiating lines.

☐ The former home of a marine snail. A smooth capsule-shaped sea shell with an elongated opening.

☐ The skeleton of a star-fish. A five-pointed, star-shaped body.

☐ Parts of the armor of a crab, shed when its owner grew too large for it. Jointed legs with claws, or a glossy shield with spines.

☐ The egg case of a flat, primitive fish called a skate. A mysterious, flattened, leathery case with two horns pointing forward and two behind.

☐ The skeleton of a sea urchin. A hard, hollow shell that looks somewhat like a flattened orange.

☐ The shelter of a marine snail called a periwinkle. A small, cone-shaped shell that looks like a sun hat.

80

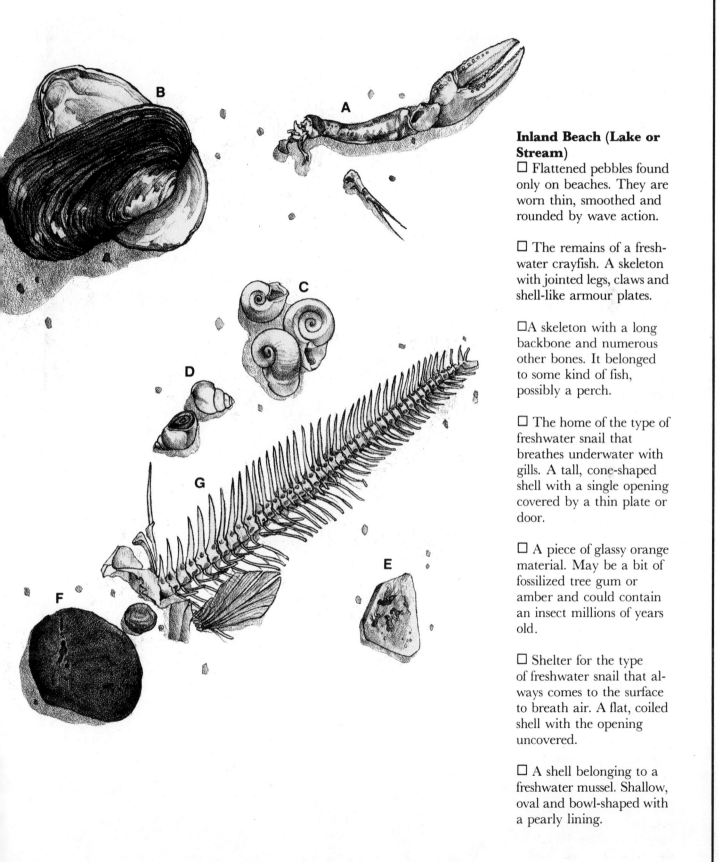

**Inland Beach (Lake or Stream)**

☐ Flattened pebbles found only on beaches. They are worn thin, smoothed and rounded by wave action.

☐ The remains of a freshwater crayfish. A skeleton with jointed legs, claws and shell-like armour plates.

☐ A skeleton with a long backbone and numerous other bones. It belonged to some kind of fish, possibly a perch.

☐ The home of the type of freshwater snail that breathes underwater with gills. A tall, cone-shaped shell with a single opening covered by a thin plate or door.

☐ A piece of glassy orange material. May be a bit of fossilized tree gum or amber and could contain an insect millions of years old.

☐ Shelter for the type of freshwater snail that always comes to the surface to breath air. A flat, coiled shell with the opening uncovered.

☐ A shell belonging to a freshwater mussel. Shallow, oval and bowl-shaped with a pearly lining.

# The Secret Picnic

## a fantasy story by James Dingwall

It was a marvelous picnic. The sky was brilliant blue and a warm September breeze rustled the first fallen leaves. My parents and little sister were off in the woods exploring, but I had eaten so much I couldn't move from the blanket we'd spread on the ground. I was happy just lying there in the sun watching a trail of ants move in for the crumbs.

The ants, however, weren't the only insects in the neighborhood. Before long, a distant cousin of theirs was hovering overhead and then it lighted on my leftover ham sandwich. It was a yellowjacket, a wasp named for the black and yellow stripes that cross its abdomen. At the back end was what I hoped was a tail but was actually a stinger that looked pretty mean.

Without moving, I hissed, "Scram! Get off my sandwich. Don't be so greedy."

It moved off the sandwich all right — now it was buzzing right in front of my nose. "It's awfully mean of you to call me greedy, you know," it said. "This is the first really decent meal I've had since I was born five months ago."

"Wait a minute," I whispered, holding both my hands tightly over my face, "I didn't mean what I said. Really! There's no way I'd want to insult *you*."

"I should hope not," the yellowjacket replied, perhaps a little less angry-sounding than before.

"All spring and summer I've just about flown my wings off. If I wasn't gathering and chewing up mouthfuls of food to take back to the nest to feed the growing larvae I was chewing up wood."

The yellowjacket was now back on the sandwich continuing to roam over the ham, and flitting lightly around the mounds of mustard.

"Why do you eat wood?" I asked.

"We don't *eat* wood," sighed the yellowjacket through a mouthful of food. "It's used to make our nest. I'm a member of the paper wasp family. Don't you even know that?"

I must confess, I did think that paper wasps were those thin, brown hornet things, and I had to admit it.

"Happens all the time," the yellowjacket exclaimed. "Fact is, all sorts of wasps make their nests out of paper. We scrape some rotten wood from a tree trunk or fence post, chew it and mix it with the saliva in our mouth, and when we spread the whole mess out to dry, it becomes thin, gray paper, perfect for nest building."

"Sounds remarkable," I said.

"Quite so," the yellowjacket replied. "You'd have to look far and wide to find another insect that devotes so much time and patience to its home building."

By this time I had almost forgotten that I was talking — actually talking — to a wasp. And I wanted to see the nest — at least from a distance. I asked if I could have a tour.

"Not possible," said the yellowjacket. "It's about a foot underground over by that maple tree with the low hanging branch."

"That's the tree I was climbing just an hour ago," I said with surprise. "I could have stepped on your nest."

"Almost did," said the yellowjacket. "Some of us were watching you."

I could only sigh with relief and mumble, "Sorry, I thought you built your colonies in trees."

"Many times we do," nodded the yellowjacket. "But just as often a queen seeks out an underground hole somewhere. She comes out of hibernation in the spring, starts digging out a hole, then when she's completed the first cells of a paper nest, she begins to lay her eggs. Once worker wasps like myself have gone through several stages and emerge from pupae, we help with the nest building and feed the young grubs or larvae as well. Those clumps you see in trees could belong to other yellowjackets or our near-relatives the bald-faced wasps. Or perhaps they even belong to germanicus wasps that are almost identical to us except for..."

Suddenly, in mid-sentence, the yellowjacket began to sputter and mutter.

"Help! Got mustard on my mandibles! Quick, do you have anything to drink around here?"

I pointed to a half-finished cup of cider. The yellowjacket flew quickly over to sip the sweet juice and within a minute was back, apologizing for leaving so abruptly. "I'm quite fond of ham, but mustard does nothing for me."

"You were telling me about the germanicus wasps," I reminded it.

"Oh yes, of course. Well, I suppose I should mention that germanicus tends to be, how should I say, a little more aggressive than the rest of us. Although at this time of year, just about any wasp you talk to is a bit grumpy — we've nothing to do really. We're out of work so to speak and hungry, too."

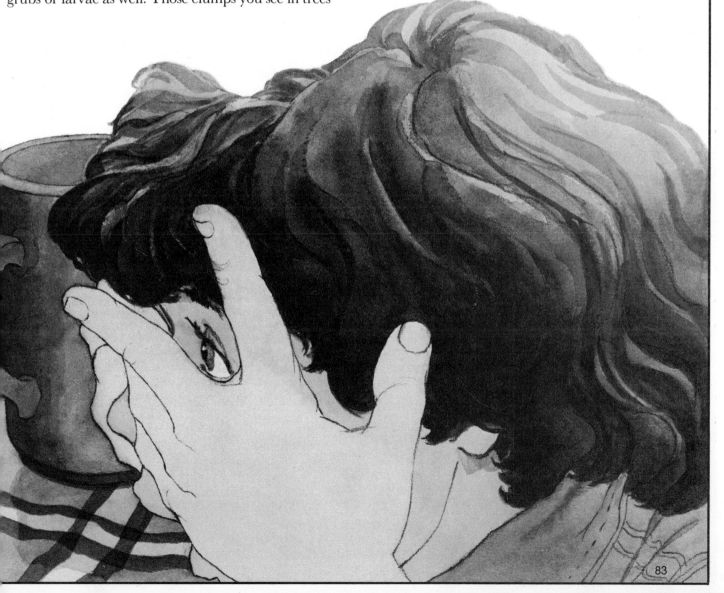

"Sounds like a bad time of year for wasps," I said, feeling rather sorry for him.

"It is, it is. By late summer, all the young wasps have changed from the pupa stage and have flown away. So there's no need for us workers to keep the nest up anymore — no one to feed or care for. And, food's getting pretty scarce too. The summer insects we used to snack on are disappearing. So we're all quite hungry. Mm-m-m. Did I tell you how much I like your sandwich?"

"Yes, you did," I said. "But, are you telling me that it's because you've nothing to do but look for food that wasps seem to be hanging around picnics more at this time of year?"

"Probably," it said, somewhat embarrassed.

"And that's why people get stung more in the fall?" I asked.

"I'm glad you brought that point up," it said, buzzing a bit. It was clearly a touchy subject for the yellowjacket.

I laughed. "On the contrary, it's you who brings the point up."

"Ohhh, bad joke," it groaned. "But it's not all our fault that these things happen."

"How so?" I wanted to know.

"Well, for one thing, look at how you and your family are out here having a picnic. Many more people than before seem to be coming to the country and when they do, they're right in our territory.

"And," it added, "when you get here, we both seem to like the same lunch: apples, grapes and luncheon meats."

"But we don't mean to hurt," I said.

"No doubt," it replied. "As people go, *you* seem quite reasonable."

"But why do you sting us?" I asked.

"Habit, I guess," was all the yellowjacket could think of. "Remember, we've spent our whole lives protecting our colony from intruders and predators. Our stinger is our only weapon."

"While we're on the subject," I said, "many people think that once you've stung you lose your stinger. Is that true?"

"Not at all," it said. "That type of thing only happens to honeybees. And I think they're one of our craziest relatives, anyway."

"Honeybees, crazy?" I asked.

"Certainly," it replied. "Not only do those foolish insects lose their stinger and die but they'll live in silly, man-made boxes making honey for every human and beast that comes along. It's truly a crazy way to live."

"That's not so crazy," I retorted. "The honeybee has a better, friendlier reputation among people than you do. What does a wasp do that equals the making of honey or pollinating flowers?"

"Look at the forest around you," sighed the yellowjacket. "I can assure you, if it weren't for the wasp populations around here, half the leaves of every tree would be eaten by caterpillars. Those slinky little things make up most of our diet during the spring and summer.

"Trouble with you humans," continued the yellowjacket with a troubled voice, "is that unless you *know* or can see what animals or insects do that is helpful to nature, you think they do nothing but make pests of themselves."

Reluctantly, I had to agree he was right about that, but before I could say so I heard my parents and little sister coming back from their walk. The wasp seemed to hear them too and without so much as a goodbye it buzzed away.

My sister ran up to me and said breathlessly: "You can't believe what we were doing! We were talking with nature."

"How did you do that?" I asked.

"Well, when the birds whistled, we'd whistle back and when the squirrels chattered, we'd chatter back. You can talk to animals, you know," she said.

"No fooling," I said. And before she could see me smiling I turned and busily began rolling up the blanket and packing away the food — making sure, of course, to leave the unfinished ham sandwich behind.

# Go Snorkeling

...and you'll be surprised at the things you'll find. On the next four pages there are tips on snorkeling plus instructions on how to make a snorkel bucket that lets you peer into the water without getting your eyelashes wet. There's also a guide to common plants and creatures to be found in waters salt and fresh...

EAT YOUR HEART OUT, JACQUES COUSTEAU!

# A Salt Water Adventure

1. When you buy or borrow a mask always test it for leaks. Press it against your face, letting the strap hang free. Breathe in. If it stays in place, it fits.

2. Before you go snorkeling, wipe some of your

*Jellyfish*
See the fringe hanging below this jellyfish? This is its tentacles which are used to capture food. Some jellyfish can give a mild sting, so watch out!

*Crab*
This crab eats almost any small animal or plant, but prefers dead ones, and shuffles sideways across the bottom looking for food. It is protected from predators by its hard shell.

*Acorn barnacles*
These white shells anchored to rocks look like miniature volcanoes. If you examine them closely you'll see thread-like tendrils sweeping the water for food particles.

*Starfish*
This strange animal moves along on hundreds of tube feet which hang beneath its five star-shaped arms. It uses these strong arms to pry open clams.

spit on the inside of the glass. Then rinse it. This helps stop your mask from fogging up.

3. Bite gently on the snorkel tube and practice breathing through it. Try this with your face in the water before you begin to swim.

4. Put on flippers in the water and walk backwards in shallow water.

5. While swimming avoid splashing (it disturbs the fish and wastes energy).

6. If a little water gets in your mask don't worry — it'll help clear fog. To remove excess water, surface and pull the mask away from your face.

7. If water gets in your breathing tube, blow out like a whale!

## Golden Rules for Safe Snorkeling
—Never snorkel alone.
—Don't go too far from shore or your boat.
—Always keep your partner in sight.
—Take your bearings often so you don't become disoriented.
—A life jacket is a good idea, and with one even a non-swimmer can have fun snorkeling.

*Sea Urchin*
If you step on this spiky animal you'll know it — so be careful! It clings or slowly crawls across rocks looking for its favorite food, sea lettuce.

*Sea Anemone*
These animals look like flowers, but are cousins of the jellyfish. Touch them and they'll pull back their tentacles into the safety of their thick stalk.

*Sea Lettuce*
This abundant green plant is the food of many marine creatures. You can recognize this tissue-paper thin plant by its bright green leafy appearance.

87

# A Fresh Water Adventure

**Dragonfly Nymph**

The adult dragonfly soars through the air eating mosquitoes, and its torpedo-shaped green or brown offspring stalks the mosquito larva (or wriggler) underwater. This carnivorous insect uses jet propulsion to escape such enemies as the sunfish.

**Crayfish**

The crayfish looks like a miniature lobster, but it won't pinch you unless you stick your fingers into its burrow under a stone. It will eat almost anything it can find.

**Eel grass**

This common water plant provides shelter for many animals.

**Minnow**

There are many kinds of minnows but they all eat tiny floating plants and aquatic insects, and are eaten by larger fishes. They are often seen in schools of up to 50 fish.

**Bladderwort**

This lacy plant is carnivorous. It has hundreds of small "purses" or traps that suck in tiny water animals on which it feeds. Despite this danger, thousands of creatures live amongst its branches.

## Make a Snorkel Bucket

Here's one way to see what's happening underwater without even getting your face wet. You will need: an empty plastic pail or a large ice cream container, a sharp knife, plastic wrap and a couple of rubber bands knotted together in a circle.

Cut out the bottom of the pail, making the hole slightly smaller than the bottom (ask an adult to help you with this), and cover the hole and the sides of the pail with a large piece of plastic wrap.

Keep the plastic wrap in place by sliding rubber bands 3/4 of the way up the side of the pail.

Use your snorkel bucket in shallow water. Push your snorkel bucket into the water but don't let any water get inside. The

pressure of the water causes the plastic to become a convex "lens" so you can see plants and animals larger than they really are.

*Diving Beetle*
There are many kinds of diving beetles that feed on insects, and sometimes even small fish. They carry a natural aqualung beneath the shiny wing covers on their backs and swim to the surface to renew their air supply.

*Leopard Frog*
This frog has the ability to be able to breathe through its nostrils in the air and through its skin in the water for a while. It is a superb swimmer and jumper, able to jump up to 14 times its own length.

*Sunfish*
The male sunfish can sometimes be spotted guarding a saucer-shaped nest in the sand where the female has laid her eggs. He fans the nest with his tail to keep the eggs clean and give them oxygen.

# The OWL Experimental Superplane

and finally along line 3.

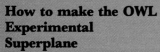

4. Fold side 2 in the same way, and you'll end up with a plane that looks like this:

5. Turn the plane over so that you can spread its wings flat on the table. Tape the wings to both sides of the body of the plane as shown:

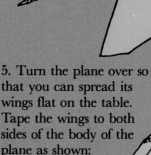

body

ta

Zoom! You've probably all made paper planes, but by using some simple aerodynamic know-how, you can make a superplane that turns, climbs, dives, rolls, even loops-the-loop. And the OWL Superplane is so super easy you'll be flying it within minutes.

nose

side 1

6. Fasten the top of the wings together, with a small piece of tape.

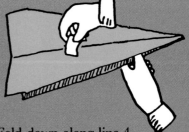

3. Starting on side 1, fold along line 1:

**How to make the OWL Experimental Superplane**

1. Cut out the plane pattern on the next page and turn it over so that the folding lines are underneath. Fold toward you along the dotted line at the top of the pattern.

2. Fold the pattern in half lengthwise so that the folding lines are inside.

then along line 2:

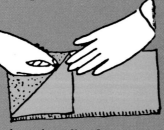

7. Fold down along line 4 on the side of each wing to make two stabilizers. Tilt the wings up slightly, hold the body where you've taped it, and your Superplane is ready to fly.

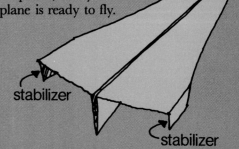

stabilizer

stabilizer

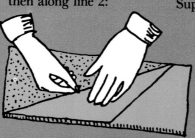

The OWL Experimental Superplane

1.

2.

3.

4.

dder   —flap——   SIDE 1   |   SIDE 2   —flap——   rudder

# Stunt Flying Your Superplane

Now that you've made your superplane and practiced flying it, it's time to learn how to make it do some stunts...

## How to make your superplane turn

On the inside of each stabilizer you'll find a dotted line. Cut along each line to make two rudders. To make your superplane turn to the right, fold in the right rudder; to go left, fold in the left rudder.

How do rudders make your superplane turn left or right? One rudder folded in acts the same way as a brake. It slows one side of the plane down, causing it to turn in that direction. (It's a bit like when you drag one foot on the ground while riding your bike.)

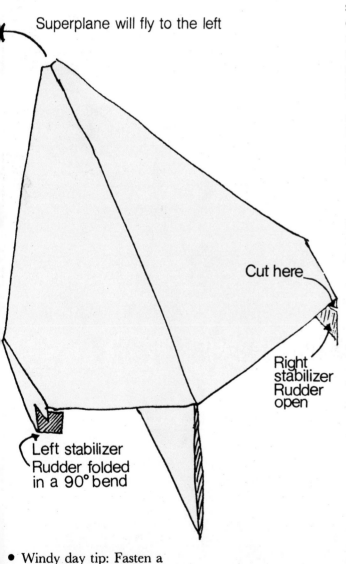

Superplane will fly to the left

Cut here

Right stabilizer Rudder open

Left stabilizer Rudder folded in a 90° bend

• Windy day tip: Fasten a paper clip to your Superplane's body near the tape. This extra weight will help keep it steady.

## How to make your superplane climb and dive

At the back of each wing you'll find four short lines. Cut along each to make two sets of flaps. When you straighten both rudders and fold these flaps up, your superplane will climb. Fold them down to make it dive.

How do flaps make the superplane climb and dive? When the flaps are up, air rushing over the top of the plane hits them and pushes the tail down, helping the nose to rise. When the flaps are down, air rushing over the bottom of the plane hits them, and pushes the tail up.

• If your superplane climbs too steeply, launch it with its nose pointing slightly down.
• If your superplane dives too much, launch it with its nose pointing slightly up.

## How to make your superplane perform a wing roll

Straighten out each rudder, then bend one flap up and the other one down. Your superplane will do a right wing roll if you fold the right flap up, and a left wing roll if you fold the left flap up.

## How to make your superplane loop-the-loop — the ace stunt!

This stunt takes a bit of practice — but it's worth it. Straighten out the

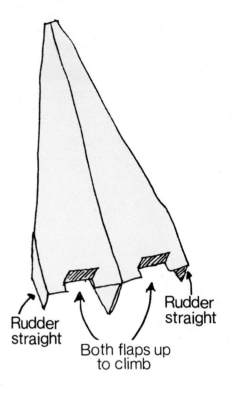

Rudder straight

Both flaps up to climb

Rudder straight

rudders and put both flaps up. Stand at the top of some steps or on a high spot so there's plenty of space for your superplane to make a complete loop in the air. Launch your superplane as hard and as fast as you can and make sure both wings are level.

## Ideas for a Backyard Stunt Competition

1. Set up an obstacle course with old tires, clotheslines, etc. that your superplane has to climb over, dive under and fly through.
2. See which of your friends can make their superplanes do the most wing rolls — in both directions.
3. See who can make their superplanes fly the farthest.
4. See who can make their superplanes do the most loop-the-loops.

# Rainy Day Album

**Need ideas to chase away the rainy day gloom? Then read on because the next six pages are crammed full of puzzles, games and things to do that are guaranteed to send the clouds away.**

*Answers on page 128.*

Here's how to make a thunderstorm of your own while you're waiting for the rain to stop. Score a square piece of cardboard with a knife from corner to corner, being careful not to cut all the way through. Turn the cardboard over and place a triangular piece of brown paper half the size of the square on it. Fold the edges over as in the illustration and tape. Now you've built your banger. Hold it above your head and fling your arm downward quickly. And you thought thunder was loud!

To find out how far away a real thunderstorm is, count the number of seconds between the lightning flash and the sound of the thunder and divide by five. This will tell you approximately how many miles away the lightning struck.

If the flash and the thunder happen together, you won't need any math to tell you that the storm's directly overhead. Your ears will be ringing!

Here's a way to send a secret message to a friend that no one (except other readers of this book) should be able to decipher. Cut out a page of newspaper that has lots of print. Then, starting at the top of the first column, spell out your message by pushing a pin through each letter as you come to it. Keep punching until your entire message is complete. To read the message your friend should hold the pinpricked paper up to the light and write down the letters you've punched in the correct order.

A totally invisible message can be sent if you write by dipping a pen into milk or lemon juice. To read the message, your friend should hold the sheet of paper over a warm lightbulb.

Lonely? Why not make some special rainy day friends by mixing a cup of flour with half a cup of salt in a large bowl and adding a third of a cup of water. Mix and you'll end up with lots of play dough to mold, roll, pat and pull into any sorts of friends you want. Paint them and leave them on the windowsill. When the sun comes out it will harden them enough to last the entire summer.

Air pollution is a very serious environmental problem. Here's a way to see for yourself just how bad it is in your area: put a clean jar outside when it's raining and bring it in when the rain is over. Fold a paper towel into a cone and pour the rain through this cone into another clean jar. Let the paper towel dry and see what you've got.

If you feel you must have a game of basketball, here's how, indoors: shape a wire coat hanger into a hoop and hang it in a door frame. Blow up a round balloon and shoot.

When you tire of balloon basketball here's a race to try: set up a race course and get your balloon from start to finish without letting it touch the ground and without using your hands.

Did you know that most kids grow more during the summer? To find out exactly how much you're sprouting, measure yourself — and your friends — right now. Then measure again once school starts.

JOHN ___

CATHY ___

DEBBIE ___

GEORGE ___

MARY ___

SALLY ___

I KNEW WE MADE THE HOOP TOO SMALL!

To make a celery stalk blush all you need to do is slice it halfway up, stand one side in a glass of plain water and the other side in a glass of water to which red food coloring has been added. Half the stalk will be blushing by morning. Do you know why?

ME ___

This is a terrific whistle to make. *But don't blow it indoors!* Cut a piece of paper into two strips 14 cm by 1.5 cm/5 in. by ½ in. Fold over 2.5 cm/1 in. on one end of each strip. Hold the strips between your fingers. Press your lips against the short flaps. Separate your fingers and blow hard.

Water can help you make a sculpture. Fill a screwtop, watertight jar halfway with water. Add drops of food coloring, then slowly fill the jar to the top with vegetable oil. Screw the lid on very tight and hold the jar sideways, then roll the jar back and forth a few times to get your sculpture moving. Why does this work? Oil is heavier than water so they can't mix.

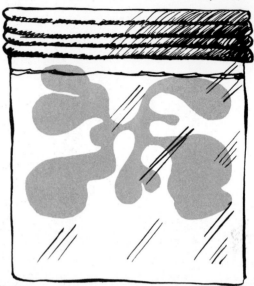

No wonder the Hatter in *Alice in Wonderland* was mad. He was probably trying to solve this puzzle invented by Lewis Carroll, the man who wrote about Alice and her adventures down the rabbit-hole. Now it's your turn to try. Can you draw the three squares in one continuous line without crossing any lines or taking your pencil off the paper?

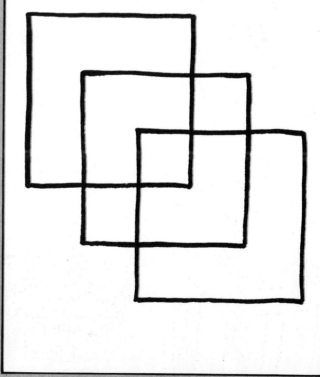

This problem might take you all summer to untangle. You'll need a friend and two pieces of string about a metre or yard long. Loosely tie your friend's wrists together with a piece of string. Loop the second string over the first string, then loosely tie your own wrists together with the second piece of string. Can you untangle yourselves without breaking or untying the string?

These word puzzles should keep you busy for quite some time. They all are ways of writing well known sayings or phrases without using all the words.

For instance:

pineapple ɔʞɐɔ

can be be interpreted to mean pineapple upside-down cake. Now try these:

---

chicken

---

V
I
O
l
e
t
s

---

symphon

---

O O O circus

---

wear

long

---

r
o
rail
d

---

The rain can paint pictures if you give it a chance. Dab different colors of paint (bright, strong colors work best) on sheets of paper, then hold them in the rain for a few seconds. Let the paper dry, then think of names for the rain's pictures.

---

How fast can you think? If you think quickly you should be able to fill in the squares below with a plant, an animal and a food beginning with each letter in the word *apricot* in no time at all. We've done a couple for you to give you a head start. Ready. Set. Go!

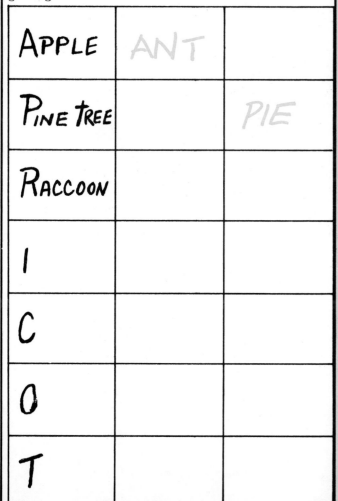

| | | |
|---|---|---|
| APPLE | ANT | |
| PINE TREE | | PIE |
| RACCOON | | |
| I | | |
| C | | |
| O | | |
| T | | |

---

There are lots of triangles in this five-sided diagram. How many can you find?

Can you rearrange these six coins to make a cross, with four coins across and four down?

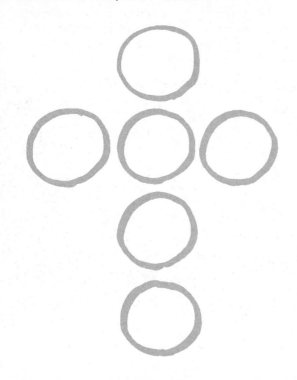

By moving only three coins can you make a triangle like this point downwards instead of up?

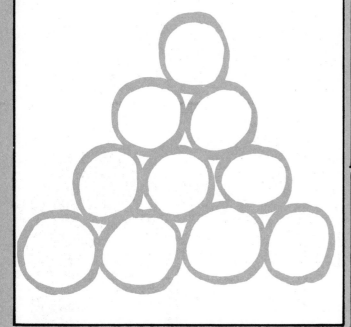

Pennies look better after a bath. To shine up your dirty old pennies, drop them in a couple of table- spoons of vinegar and a few pinches of salt. Rinse the pennies in water and dry them with a paper towel.

Here's a whirly swirly bird to twirl. To make it, you need stiff paper 8 cm by 5 cm/3 in. by 2 in., a toothpick, scissors, tape and a cork. Cut the paper as shown and tape on a toothpick. Bend the paper and push the toothpick into the cork. Stand on a sturdy chair and let your bird drop.

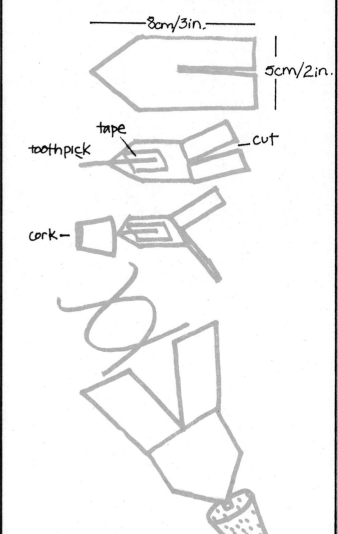

These dots can be connect- ed with straight lines to make a perfect cross that has five dots inside it and eight dots outside. Can you do it?

Can you take away just one toothpick and leave exactly three squares?

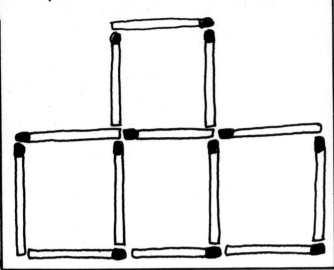

Copy this drawing on a large sheet of paper and then cut it out. Mix up the pieces and challenge your friend to put them together so they make a square.

Here's an interesting race to have with a friend. See who can write down the most words that rhyme with the word "red" in two minutes.

If your phone number were 468-3297 it would spell "hot days." It's true! Look at the letters that go with each number on your telephone dial or the push buttons. See if your real phone number spells something. Were you lucky? Now how about your friends and relatives?

## Glare Goggles

Learn from the native people who live in the North and make some sun goggles. Theirs were made out of whale bones but heavy cardboard 15 cm by 5 cm/6 in. by 2 in. will do just as well. You'll also need a ruler, a pencil, 2 pieces of string to go around your head, colored markers or crayons.

1. Hold the cardboard up to your face so a friend can mark the spots for your eyes.
2. Using a pencil and a ruler draw two slits.
3. Cut out the slits with scissors.
4. Make a notch for your nose.
5. Poke a hole in either side of the goggles, loop a string through each and tie it. Color your goggles with your own design and they're ready to wear.

# Your Bike Up Close

How well do you know your bicycle? You probably know where the saddle, handlebars and pedals are, but what about the chain stays, crank or the hand tube? The parts of a bicycle are numbered below. How many can you put in the right place?

*Answers on page 128*

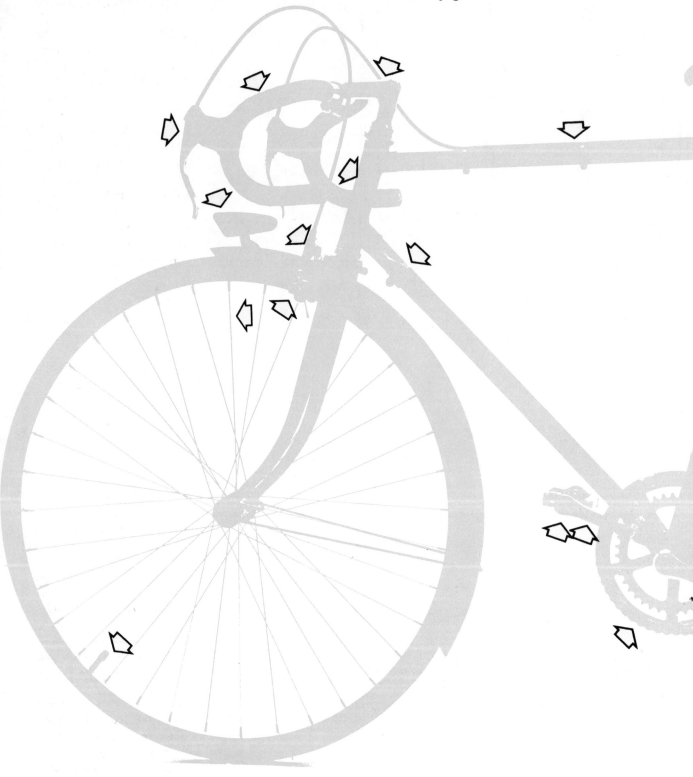

1. front light
2. brake levers
3. handlebar extension
4. handlebars

5. seat tube
6. saddle
7. crossbar
8. chain stays

9. rear brake
10. valve
11. spoke
12. mudguards

13. rear light
14. chainwheel
15. pedal
16. crank

17. rear derailleur
18. front derailleur
19. seat post
20. gear change levers

21. head tube
22. front brake
23. brake pads

## Tips to keep your bike in tune

If your bike is running smoothly, you can get where you're going five times faster than walking.

1. Wash your bike at least once a month with warm soapy water and a stiff brush. This not only keeps it looking pretty but will prevent it from rusting. Rinse the soap off with clean water and dry.

2. Anything that moves needs oil, so squirt a drop of oil on *all* your bike's moving parts monthly. Any light machine oil or bike oil will do, but take care not to get any oil on the tires and wheel rims or your brakes might slip.

3. One of the most important maintenance tips is to keep your chain clean. Wipe it once a week with an old rag then give it a squirt of oil on the side that meets the gears. Once a year clean the chain with an old toothbrush.

4. Is there enough air in your tires? If they're properly filled, it's easier to pedal. Have a service station attendant help you fill your tires to the correct pressure for you.

5. Now that you're ready to roll fast, think about how you'll stop. Are the brake pads of your hand brakes worn? If so, have them replaced. And make sure that they grip the wheel rims — not the tires — tightly.

6. While doing this inspection, make sure all nuts and bolts on your bike are screwed on tightly.

7. If you're going away for a few weeks or putting your bike away for the winter, either stand it upside down or hang it from large hooks.

# BLACKTOP STUNT SHOW

Of course you know that only a small part of your bike's tires touch the ground at any one time, but did you know that each wheel balances on a space that's smaller than the size of a small chocolate bar? Isn't it amazing that it's so easy to balance on these small spaces when you are bicycling fast?

To put this new knowledge — and your riding skills — to the test why not organize a special schoolyard or park stunt show with some friends. Here are a few events; you'll no doubt be able to think of many more. Bring along an adult to be judge and safety official.

## Zeroing In

See if you can ride from the outside to the inside of a spiral that has been drawn on the ground without putting your foot down or touching the chalk lines. Try one race fast, another slow. Hot riders can try starting from the center of the spiral and riding outwards.

## Hill Climb

You need a steep hill for this activity and plenty of energy. At the starting whistle pedal as hard as you can up the hill. Whoever gets to the top of the hill first, is the winner.

## Pedal Pedal Bang Bang

This is a good event if you have 30 balloons or so left over from a party. The rider who breaks the least number of balloons and keeps within the boundaries for a set time limit — say three minutes — wins.

## Bike Basketball

With practice, you'll be able to form your own Globetrotter team. You need as many balls as you can carry (tennis balls will do), with the same number of baskets. The winner is the rider who makes the most baskets in the least amount of time.

## Bookmobile

Discover how far you can ride with a book balanced up top. (Use an old book as it's certain to drop.)

## Z-Z-Z-O-O-O-M-M

At the starting whistle pedal as hard as you can. Once you pass the marker you must coast. Whoever coasts the farthest is the winner.

# Unboring Things to Do

**Now you have no excuse for twiddling your thumbs. What follows are terrific ideas for an unboring spring, summer and fall.**

*Answers to puzzles are on page 128.*

Sunflowers are easy to grow and will attract birds to your garden. Plant seeds (not roasted ones) outside in a sunny place. Water well and check every day that the soil is moist. Sunflowers grow quickly and they should be taller than you by the end of summer. Then you can reach up and pick the seeds. They're great roasted in the oven.

Lift a stone and see who lives underneath. But don't forget to put the rock back.

Drop a bit of honey or a crumb in an ant's path. Does it get the food home? How? Then try running your finger across its trail and see what it does when it reaches your scent.

Instead of just picking off those prickly burrs from your laces and socks, save them to make "burry" animals. For a terrific burr bear, use a big burr to make a head, lots of little burrs for legs and arms.

Tear a small hole in a spider web and watch what happens. What does the spider do?

Follow the cat for the afternoon. Be prepared to go slowly and let the cat be the leader. Get ready to climb fences and pause sometimes to sniff. You'll see your neighborhood through a pair of new eyes.

Hunt for shells (there are more than 100,000 kinds in the world) along the shores of oceans, lakes or rivers. Sometimes they're buried in sand or mud and you have to dig for them. Get a shell book from the library to help you identify them. After cleaning the shells make a shell necklace by stringing the shells together on a thick thread, or collect them in glass jars or even glue them together to make strange creatures or animals.

Take any animal's footprints home with you — All you'll need are:

bucket
stirring stick
water
plaster of Paris
narrow cardboard
   strip long enough to fit
   around the track

1. Press the cardboard strip upright in the ground to form a collar around the track.

2. Pour water into your bucket and add plaster of Paris and stir until the mixture is smooth.
3. Pour the plaster into the circle about 2.5 cm/1 in. thick. Let it dry — this may take a couple of hours.
4. Carefully lift up the cardboard collar with the plaster cast inside.
5. Brush off any mud and paint your cast if you want. If you don't know what animal made the track, a track book from the library might help.

Make a sundial the easy way. Place a garden stake or a medium-sized stick in the ground, making sure there's lots of clear space around it. Start in the early morning on a sunny day and mark with smaller stakes the tip of the shadow cast by the larger stick every hour on the hour until you have staked out all the daylight hours.

Find out which animals prowl around your home at night. Choose a space between your home and some trees and late in the day cover it with sand. Wet the sand and smooth it out by drawing a piece of wood over it so you have a path about a few steps wide and as long as you like. Place a bowl of water and some food (such as scraps, seeds, fruit, nuts and bread) on the side of the "track" patch that's closest to your house. Get up early the next day and see if you can identify the animals that ate your food by the tracks they left. They could include raccoons, chipmunks, fox and mice. A track book from the library might help.

Here's something nice and messy to do — making balloons into weird creatures with papier-mâché. You'll need:

small round balloons
lots of newspapers torn
   into small strips
a large flat-bottomed
   dish
¾ cup white flour
1 1/3 cups warm water
wax paper
paints, brushes, seeds,
   strings, buttons, etc.
glue

1. Put the flour in the flat-bottomed dish and add the warm water. Mix it into a smooth paste with your fingers. You might need to make more glue as you go along.
2. Blow up a balloon and knot the end.
3. Paste the pieces of newspaper onto the balloon until it is completely covered.
4. Build up the layers of paper on the balloon — you might need 10 or 12.
5. Using more paper and paste, carefully mould your creature's nose, ears, feet, whatever, and paste them onto the balloon.
6. Sit the balloon in the sun on a sheet of wax paper and let it dry completely.
7. Paint the balloon, add buttons or seeds for eyes — now let your imagination run wild.

Here are two ways for you and a friend to make a unique portrait of yourselves:
1. In the early morning or late evening, tape a large piece of paper on the ground. Stand so your shadow falls on the paper and have your friend trace your outline. Then color, paint or do whatever you like with it, including making a collage of leaves, seeds or feathers within its borders.
2. Try this again at noon and see how different your drawings become when the sun is in a different position in the sky.

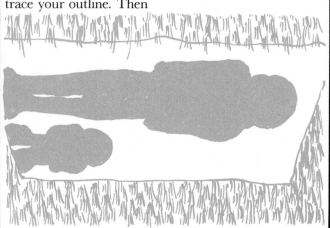

Walk taller on a couple of large empty juice cans. Use a hammer and nail to make two holes opposite each other in each can. Attach two ropes long enough to hold easily in your hands. Hold the ropes tightly to keep your balance and away you go.

Color your own sand by simply adding several drops of food coloring. Screw the lid on the jar and shake until the sand is completely colored. Dump the sand on newspaper and spread it around to dry. Use your colored sand to make sand paintings by brushing a mixture of water and some white glue onto a light piece of cardboard. Sprinkle sand on the glue, let it dry and shake off the extra sand.

Make sand squiggle pictures by squirting white glue on colored paper. Make swirls, designs, or write your name. Sprinkle sand all over the paper. Let the glue dry until it feels hard when you touch it. Shake off the loose sand and presto — you have a sand squiggle.

Put layers of different colored sand into a clear, wide-mouthed jar for unusual jar art. Remember to put the lid on the jar. A good shake will give you a colorful design.

Collect rubber bands, string or aluminum foil and roll them into a ball. See how big you can make your ball by the end of summer. One man, according to the *Guinness Book of World Records* made a ball 3.3m/11 ft. tall!

Explore things close up by making your own magnifying glass. You'll need:
a piece of stiff cardboard
scissors
clear plastic wrap
sticky tape
drop of water

1. Cut out a magnifying glass shape from the cardboard.
2. Stretch the piece of plastic wrap over the hole and hold it in place with tape.
3. Put a drop of water on the plastic and — voilà — a magnifying glass.

Collect as many different kinds of leaves as you can find. Press them in a book between sheets of wax paper.

Collect rocks and oddly shaped stones. With just paints and a brush you can turn your collection into a set of crazy creatures and people.

# Meet the BEETLES

Watch out — these tiger beetles crawling towards you are ferocious hunters!

Fortunately — unless you're smaller than a pea — you're in no danger. In fact, if you are bigger than a pea, you can discover that beetles are beautiful to look at ...

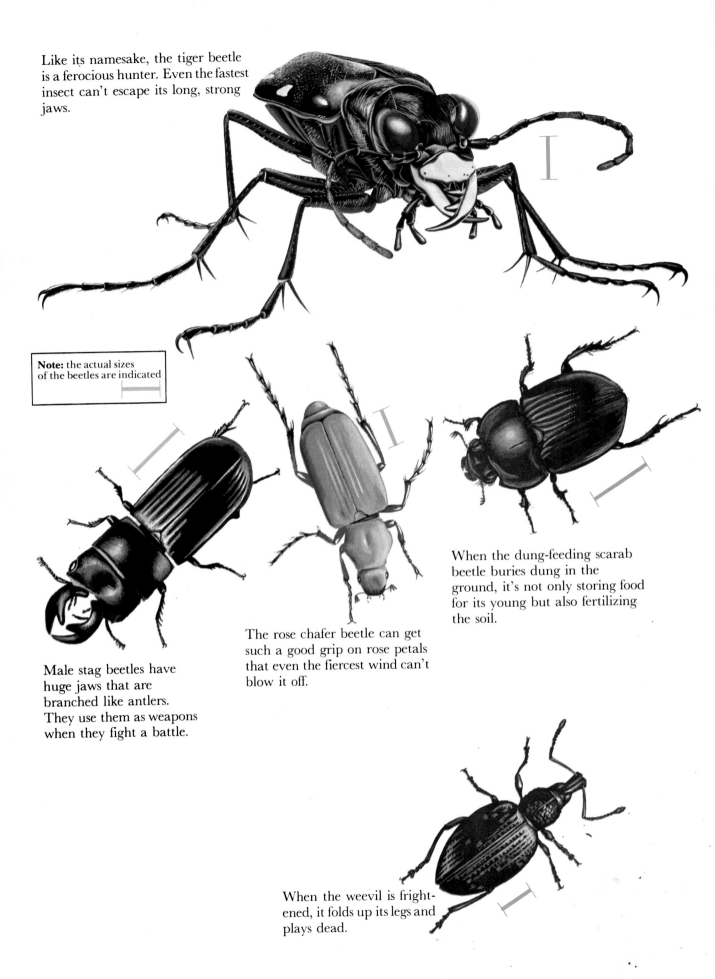

Like its namesake, the tiger beetle is a ferocious hunter. Even the fastest insect can't escape its long, strong jaws.

**Note:** the actual sizes of the beetles are indicated

Male stag beetles have huge jaws that are branched like antlers. They use them as weapons when they fight a battle.

The rose chafer beetle can get such a good grip on rose petals that even the fiercest wind can't blow it off.

When the dung-feeding scarab beetle buries dung in the ground, it's not only storing food for its young but also fertilizing the soil.

When the weevil is frightened, it folds up its legs and plays dead.

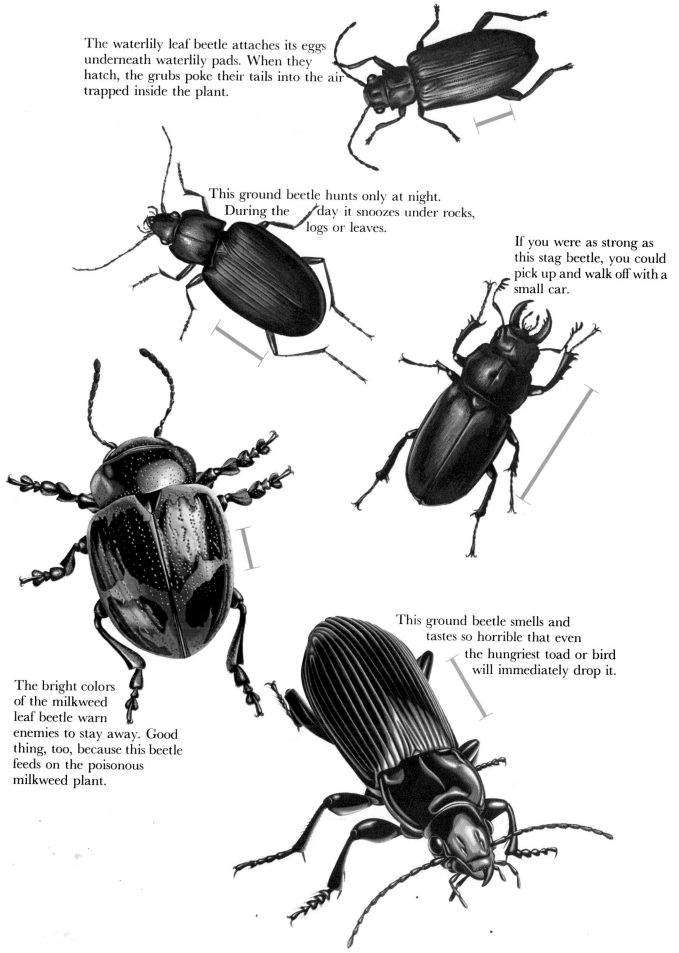

The waterlily leaf beetle attaches its eggs underneath waterlily pads. When they hatch, the grubs poke their tails into the air trapped inside the plant.

This ground beetle hunts only at night. During the day it snoozes under rocks, logs or leaves.

If you were as strong as this stag beetle, you could pick up and walk off with a small car.

The bright colors of the milkweed leaf beetle warn enemies to stay away. Good thing, too, because this beetle feeds on the poisonous milkweed plant.

This ground beetle smells and tastes so horrible that even the hungriest toad or bird will immediately drop it.

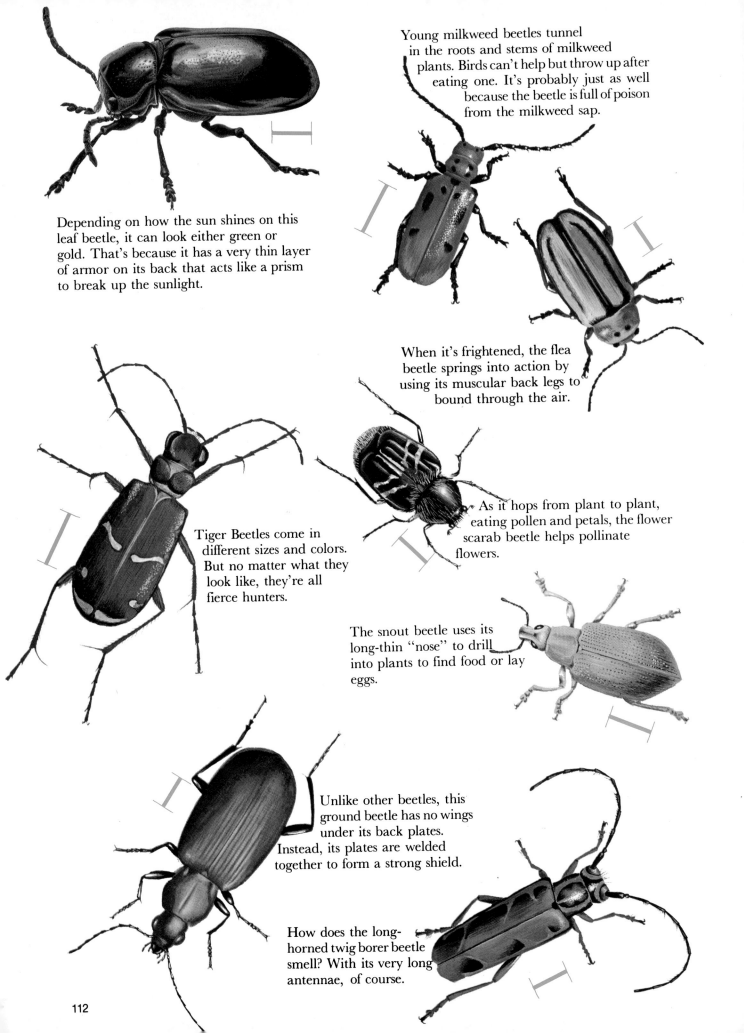

Depending on how the sun shines on this leaf beetle, it can look either green or gold. That's because it has a very thin layer of armor on its back that acts like a prism to break up the sunlight.

Young milkweed beetles tunnel in the roots and stems of milkweed plants. Birds can't help but throw up after eating one. It's probably just as well because the beetle is full of poison from the milkweed sap.

When it's frightened, the flea beetle springs into action by using its muscular back legs to bound through the air.

Tiger Beetles come in different sizes and colors. But no matter what they look like, they're all fierce hunters.

As it hops from plant to plant, eating pollen and petals, the flower scarab beetle helps pollinate flowers.

The snout beetle uses its long-thin "nose" to drill into plants to find food or lay eggs.

Unlike other beetles, this ground beetle has no wings under its back plates. Instead, its plates are welded together to form a strong shield.

How does the long-horned twig borer beetle smell? With its very long antennae, of course.

# Beetlemania Box Score

Here's a handy chart to keep track of all the beetles you might spot this summer. This will make a terrific school project too.

**Interesting Beetles I've Seen**

Name of Beetle _____

What it looked like _____

When I saw it _____

What it was doing _____

_____

**Interesting Beetles I've Seen**

Name of Beetle _____

What it looked like _____

When I saw it _____

What it was doing _____

_____

**Interesting Beetles I've Seen**

Name of Beetle _____

What it looked like _____

When I saw it _____

What it was doing _____

_____

**Interesting Beetles I've Seen**

Name of Beetle _____

What it looked like _____

When I saw it _____

What it was doing _____

_____

**Interesting Beetles I've Seen**

Name of Beetle _____

What it looked like _____

When I saw it _____

What it was doing _____

_____

**Interesting Beetles I've Seen**

Name of Beetle _____

What it looked like _____

When I saw it _____

What it was doing _____

_____

**Interesting Beetles I've Seen**

Name of Beetle _____

What it looked like _____

When I saw it _____

What it was doing _____

_____

**Interesting Beetles I've Seen**

Name of Beetle _____

What it looked like _____

When I saw it _____

What it was doing _____

_____

# Orienteering

More and more kids and adults are becoming excited about orienteering. It's like a huge outdoor game. Enthusiasts love it because it not only involves getting out into the countryside but requires matching wits and skills with other people in an exciting race from checkpoint to checkpoint.

Those who are quick-footed and able to use their heads to figure out the best route from point to point have the advantage.

To go orienteering, you must be able to read a map intelligently and imaginatively. A map is a wonderful source of information that allows you, if you know how to read it, to have as clear a picture of unknown territory as if you were actually there. A map, for example, can tell you the location of a hill that is so steep it defies climbing, or marshy ground that is virtually impassable. Here are some tips to help you get a better understanding of maps.

1. To read a map well you need to know these symbols by memory. Practice by covering up the words and trying to locate and identify these symbols on the map opposite.

2. Contour lines like this indicate hills and valleys. The space between the lines (called the "contour interval") is three metres or about nine feet. Therefore the closer the lines the steeper the hill.

dirt road

distinct trail

indistinct trail

buildings

crossable stream

spring

ruin

boulder

cliff hang

dense forest

semi-open areas

beaver dam

marsh, uncrossable

marsh, crossable, open

lake, uncrossable

swampy forest, crossable

If you've successfully found all the things above on the map you know some of the basics of map reading. Are you ready to go on and play the "Great Orienteering Game" on the next page? Ready, set, go!

114

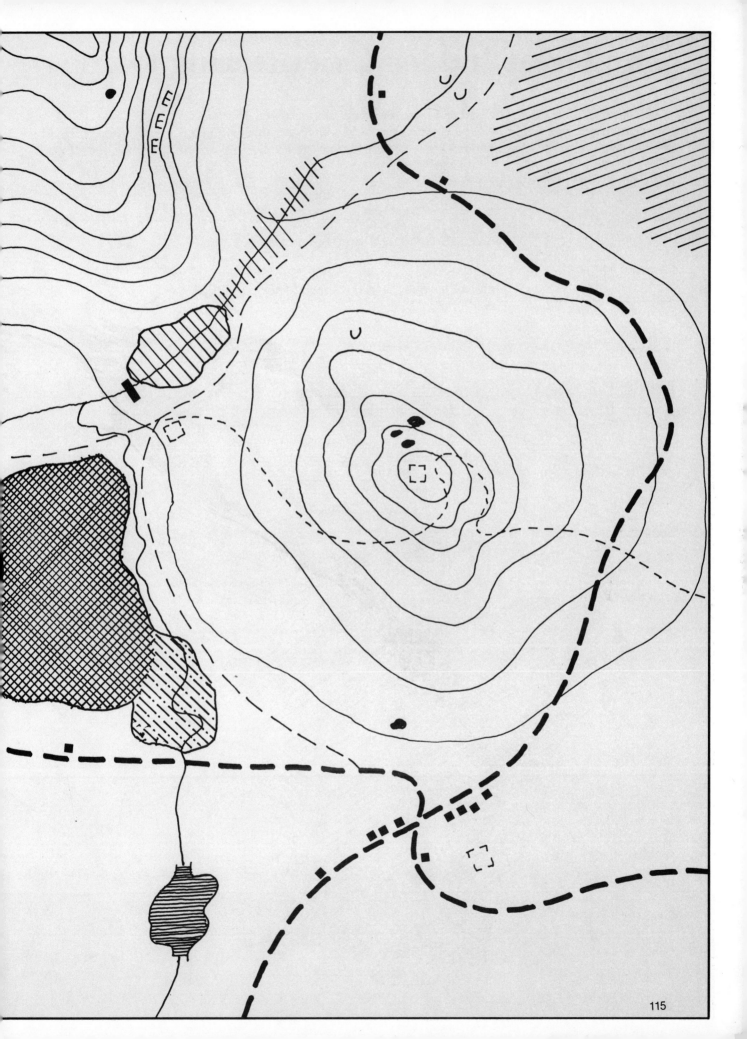

115

# The Great Indoor Orienteering Game

The object of this game is to begin at checkpoint A on the map and get to checkpoints B and C in order by the best route. If you play with a friend time your trips to see who was the fastest.

Tips: Use the map-reading skills you have learned, and read the map carefully to find the fastest and the easiest way.

It is better to go around a steep hill than to try to climb it. You obviously can only cross a river or a marsh that is shown as crossable. But look carefully at seemingly formidable land features — they may be more passable than you think.

Open areas often provide the easiest route but not necessarily the fastest.

Before you make your choice of route study the map carefully. And good luck!

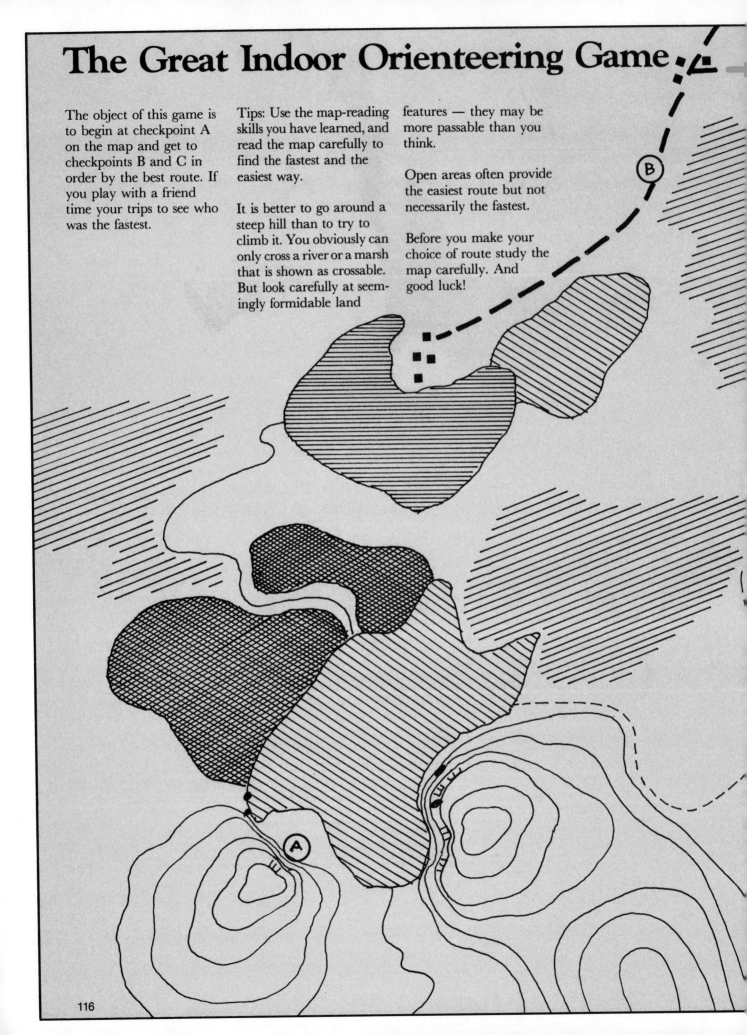

# Amazing But True

Next time you eat a watermelon, think about this! Watermelons found along the Tigris River in Iraq can weigh as much as a baby African elephant. That's big enough to feed about 250 people.

One mighty dinosaur — Stegosaurus, which roamed North America 140 million years ago — had an unusual way of keeping cool. The upright plates along its back were full of tiny blood vessels. Scientists think that when it was hot, Stegosaurus could flap its plates, which helped heat escape into the air from these blood vessels.

If you ever get lost in a desert in the hot summer sun look for the saguaro plant. It's the one that looks like a tall man waving his arms. The saguaro is the desert's biggest water storage "tank" growing as high as a five-story building.

If nothing ever seems to go right for you on hot sticky days, some scientists are saying it may not be all your fault. There are more crimes, more accidents and more mistakes made in extremely hot weather — even kids act up more in schools. Scientists think that it might have something to do with increased electrical activity in our brains, which somehow affects the way we act.

Lightning does strike the same place twice, especially tall objects such as trees, mountain tops and buildings. The 600 m/ 1,920 ft. tall CN Tower in Toronto, Canada, is hit by lightning up to 200 times a year. Right this very minute there are 2,000 thunderstorms raging around the world. A lightning bolt is more than four times hotter than the surface of the sun.

Some plants survive the brief arctic summer season in a most efficient way. The arctic poppy, for instance, works like a mini-solar heater. Its flower always turns to face the sun and the petals act like reflectors focusing heat toward the middle of the flower. If the arctic poppy didn't behave in this way, it would not get enough heat for its seeds to ripen.

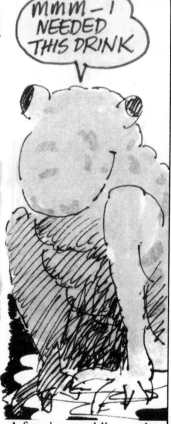

The knobcone pine loves forest fires. That's because its seed-filled cones only pop when they're fire-hot. And if they pop and fall on fertile ground, new little knobcone pines will grow.

A frog in a puddle on a hot day is quenching its thirst even if its mouth is firmly shut. How? It "drinks" through its skin.

Next time you dip into a large jar of honey, give a thought to the 80,000 bees that flew the equivalent of three times around the world to gather the nectar needed to make enough honey to fill it.

# Boats to Build

You can be every inch a sailor with these easy-to-build boats. Then head to the beach or fill your wading pool and sail away!

### S.S. Delta Cow

For two boats, you will need:
an empty 500 mL/pint
  milk carton
scissors
four pencils longer than
  the milk carton
two strong rubber bands
a popsicle stick broken
  in two

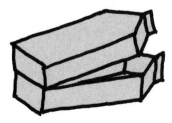

1. Get an adult to help you punch a hole in the middle of one side of the carton.
2. Cut the milk carton in half, as in the illustration, to make a hull for each boat. Set one half aside.

3. Insert pencils.

4. Knot a small loop near the end of a rubber band. Put the popsicle stick in this loop.

5. Slip the rubber band over the pencils so that the propeller is in the middle.

6. Make another boat with the other half of the carton. Find a friend and have a race.

## Super Sailboat

You'll need an adult to help you make this boat. To make your sailboat you will need:

wood for the hull
cloth for the sail
dowelling for the
    mast and boom
string
tape
saw
sandpaper
drill
white glue

**2.** Follow the diagram for the sail.

**3.** Tie the mast and boom together with string. Tape the sail to the boom and mast. Use glue to fasten the mast into the hole in the hull and — *bon voyage*.

**1.** Follow the diagram for the hull. Saw on the dotted lines. Smooth the edges with sandpaper. Have an adult drill a hole for the mast.

P.S. You can make simpler sailboats that are just as much fun to sail. Build a hull with a milk carton, plastic dish or drinking straws tied together. Use modeling clay to hold up the mast. Add a paper sail and away you go.

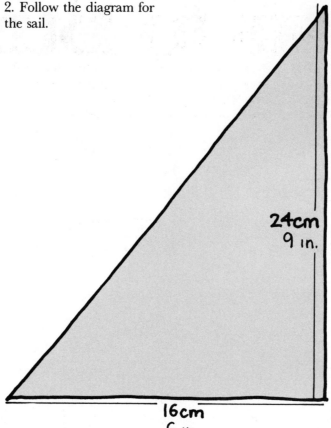

24cm
9 in.

16cm
6 in.

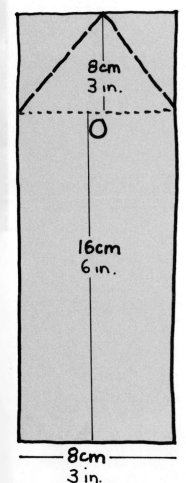

8cm
3 in.

16cm
6 in.

8cm
3 in.

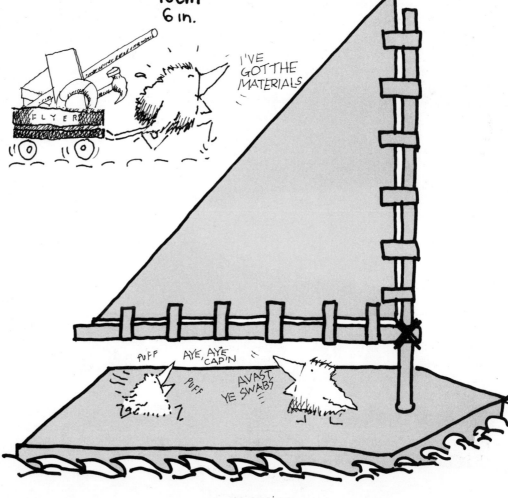

I'VE GOT THE MATERIALS

FLYER

PUFF   AYE, AYE, CAP'N
PUFF   AVAST YE SWABS

## S.S. Extra
This boat is big news anytime.
All you need to make it is a
sheet of newspaper.

1. Fold one sheet of newspaper in half like this:

2. Fold the top corners so they
meet.

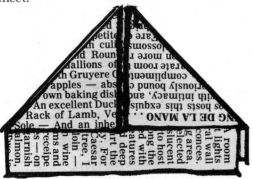

3. Fold up both edges.

**4. Bring the ends together and flatten the paper sideways.**

**5. Turn up the corners like this:**

**6. Bring the ends together and flatten the paper sideways.**

**7. Gently pull the ends open to get a great boat.**

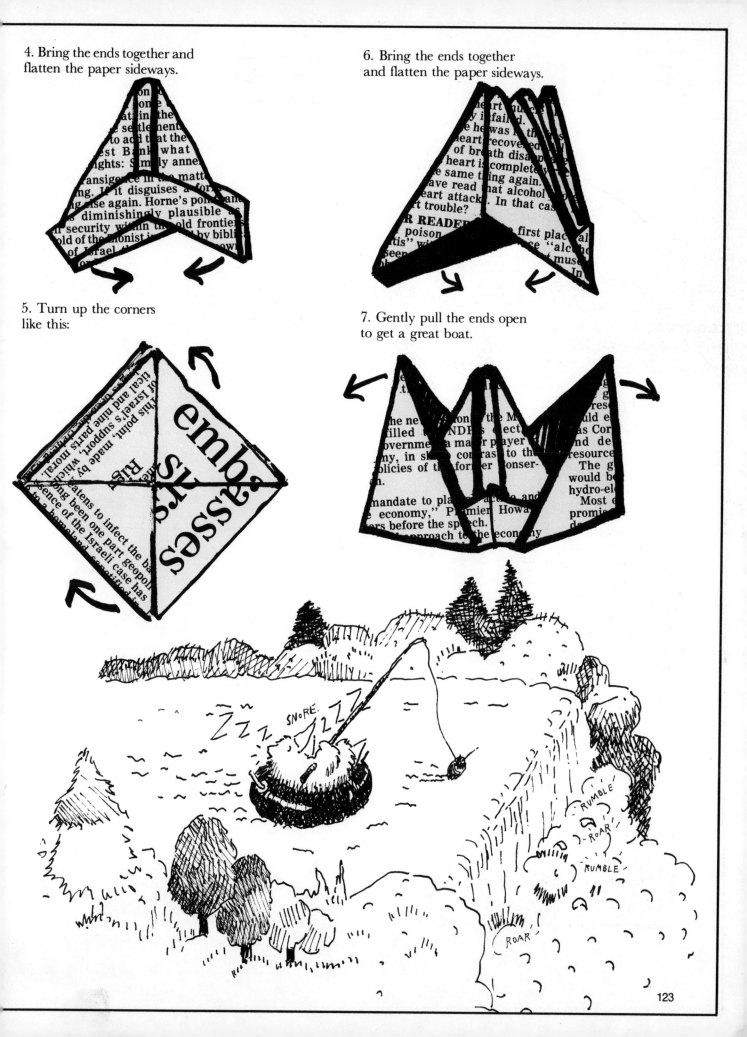

# Weed Patch Safari

Imagine that you are on a safari. You creep carefully through tall grasses and suddenly in front of you looms a ferocious-looking creature that you've never seen before. Going on an exciting "mysterious creature safari" this summer is easier than you think, and you don't even

have to leave your neighborhood. Simply lie face down in a bed of weeds or a clump of grass and peep through the blades of grass. If you have a magnifying glass, all the better. You'll find all sorts of weird and wonderful creatures.

Start your safari in this weed patch below. There are 23 different creatures here. How many can you find and identify?

*Answers on page 128*

# Be a "Signs of Autumn" Detective

How sharp a detective are you? Here is an imaginary farm scene in the late afternoon on an autumn day. There are at least 12 things going on that tell you autumn has arrived. The swallows, for example, are gathering on a fence. How many more autumn signs can you find?

*Answers on page 128*

# Answers

**Answers to Rainy Day Album on pages 94 to 101.**

## Answers to Be a "Signs of Summer" Detective on pages 8-9

The early flowers have disappeared and tulips (1) and dandelions (2) are blooming in the grass. The birch (3) and the maple (4) have leaves. Butterflies (5) have appeared, and the cat (6) is now enjoying the sun. The robin (7) is feeding its young. The rosebush (8) is uncovered, summer screens (9) are on the windows, the dog now lives outside in its kennel (10), leaves are raked up (11), the washing is on the line (12), and the swing (13) is back on the tree. Enjoying the lovely weather are the children (14) in light clothes, playing outside.

## Answers to Holiday Crossword on page 16

*Across:* 1. picnics, 5. shore, 7. dandelion, 10. lie, 12. snorkel, 13. minnow, 16. eat, 19. fishing, 21. shell, 23. bee, 24. evaporate, 25. deep

*Down:* 1. paddle, 2. canoe, 3. ice, 4. swimming, 5. sun, 6. bicycle, 8. bucket, 9. showers, 11. pail, 12. swing, 14. bubble, 15. life, 17. chair, 18. slide, 20. nest, 22. head

## Answer to Holiday Word Search on page 29

It is not true that falling raindrops are shaped like tears. Small raindrops are round while large ones are shaped like hamburger buns. They are flat on the bottom and rounded on the top.

## Answers to "Be a Cloud Detective" on pages 14/15

1. Cumulonimbus, 2. Thunderhead, 3. Cirrus, 4. Altocumulus, 5. Cirrocumulus, 6. Mammotocumulus, 7. Fair weather cumulus

## Answers to How to be a Beach Detective on pages 80/81

4 Sand dollar, 6 Marine snail, 2 Starfish, 3 Crab, 1 Skate egg case, 5 Sea urchin, 7 Periwinkle F Pebbles, A Crayfish, G Fish skeleton, D Freshwater snail with gills, E Amber or tree gum, C Air-breathing freshwater snail, B Freshwater mussel

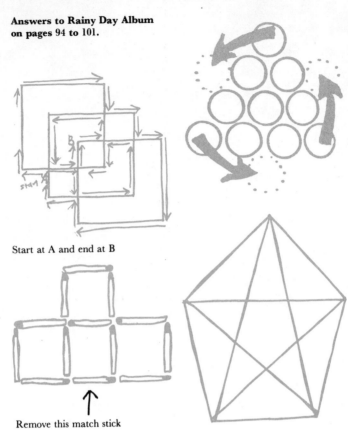

Start at A and end at B

Remove this match stick

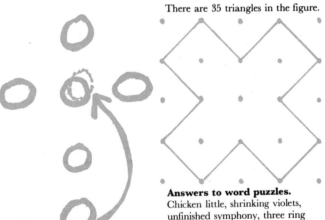

There are 35 triangles in the figure.

## Answers to word puzzles.

Chicken little, shrinking violets, unfinished symphony, three ring circus, long underwear, railroad crossing

## Answers to "Your Bike Up Close" on pages 102/103

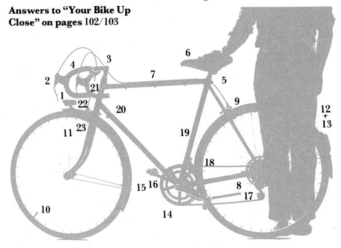

## Answers to Weedpatch Safari on pages 124/125

The following creatures are hiding in this scene: earwig, froghopper larvae, adult froghopper, grass mites, ground beetle, sow bug, black fly, millipede, American toad, praying mantis, katydid, field mouse, eastern garter snake, woolly caterpillar, garden spider, honeybee, ladybird beetle, black ants, aphids, green lacewing, mosquito, daddy longlegs, monarch butterfly

## Answers to Be a "Signs of Autumn" Detective on pages 126-127

1. Swallows are gathering on wire fences. 2. Geese are flying south. 3. The sun is low in the sky and the shadows are long. 4. One field is being tilled for planting wheat. 5. Summer screens are being removed from the house. 6. Pumpkins are being harvested. 7. Apples are ripe for picking. 8. The starling is in its speckled winter feathers. 9. Milkweed seed pods have burst. 10. Leaves are falling. 11. The oak tree has acorns. 12. The squirrel is collecting nuts for its winter food pile.

## CREDITS

pp. 8/9 Elaine Macpherson, 10/11 Photographs courtesy of Atmospheric Environment Service, 16 Chris Middleton, 17 Wasyl Szkodzinsky (Photo Researchers, Inc.), 18/19 Chris Malazdrewicz (Valan Photos), John Henry Sullivan, Jr. (Photo Researchers, Inc.), Val and J. Allan Wilkinson (Valan Photos), 20 Bruce Roberts (Photo Researchers, Inc.), Val Wilkinson (Valan Photos), Stan Pantovio (Photo Researchers, Inc.) 21/28 Linda Bucholtz, 32/33 Tina Holdcroft, 36/39 Anker Odum, 40/41 Olena Kassian, 44 Tony Thomas, 48/55 Alan Daniel, 56/57 Normunds Berzins, Clive Dobson, 61 Stan Wayman (Photo Researchers, Inc.) 62/63 Jason Rubinsteen, Maurice R. Castagne (Photo Researchers, Inc.), J. Allan Wilkinson (Valan Photos), 64/65 Tom McHugh (Photo Researchers, Inc.), Paul L. Janosi (Valan Photos), Jason Rubinsteen, 66/67 Elisabeth Weiland (Photo Researchers, Inc.), Roger Tory Peterson (Photo Researchers, Inc.), J. Allan Wilkinson (Valan Photos), J.D. Taylor (Valan Photos), 68 Jack Fields (Photo Researchers, Inc.), 78 Elaine Macpherson, 79 Tony Thomas, 82/84 Alan Daniel, 85 Tony Thomas, 86/89 Elaine Macpherson, 102/103 Tony Thomas, 109/112 Julian Mulock, 120 Linda Bucholtz, 124/127 Elaine Macpherson Cover Illustration by Lynda Cooper Acknowledgements Design Director: Nick Milton. Cover Design: Elaine Groh. Special thanks to Edith Davis, Sylvia Funston and Lyn Thomas.